E242
EDUCATION: A SECOND-LEVEL C

LEARNING FOR ALL

UNIT 1/2

MAKING CONNECTIONS

Prepared for the course team by
Tony Booth

The Open
University

E242 COURSE READERS

There are two course readers associated with E242; they are:
BOOTH, T., SWANN, W., MASTERTON, M. and POTTS, P. (eds) (1992) *Learning for All 1: curricula for diversity in education*, London, Routledge (**Reader 1**).

BOOTH, T., SWANN, W., MASTERTON, M. and POTTS, P. (eds) (1992) *Learning for All 2: policies for diversity in education*, London, Routledge (**Reader 2**).

TELEVISION PROGRAMMES AND AUDIO-CASSETTES

There are eight TV programmes and two audio-cassettes associated with E242. They are closely integrated into the unit texts and there are no separate TV or cassette notes. However, further information about them may be obtained by writing to Open University Educational Enterprises Ltd, 12 Cofferidge Close, Stony Stratford, Milton Keynes MK11 1BY.

The cover illustration shows a detail of 'Midsummer Fair' by Dorothy Bordass.

The Open University, Walton Hall, Milton Keynes MK7 6AA

First published 1992

Revised edition published 1996

Edited, designed and typeset by The Open University

Printed in the United Kingdom by Page Bros, Norwich

ISBN 0 7492 4554 9

This unit forms part of an Open University course; the complete list of units is printed at the end of this book. If you have not enrolled on the course and would like to buy this or other Open University material, please write to Open University Educational Enterprises Ltd, 12 Cofferidge Close, Stony Stratford MK11 1BY, Great Britain. If you wish to enquire about enrolling as an Open University student please write to the Admissions Office, The Open University, PO Box 48, Walton Hall, Milton Keynes MK7 6AB, Great Britain.

CONTENTS

1 INTRODUCTION

1.1 Schools contain children and young people who differ in background, attainments and interests. How should they respond to the diversity of their students?

An assembly

1.2 It is the start of the school day at the Grove, a primary school which you will visit again later in this unit when the pupils are a year older. A teacher has been working with her class of ten-year-olds preparing for an assembly. They have come to present an improvised morality play based on a traditional story and to read poems they have written. They start with the play.

1.3 The scene is a cottage last thing at night. A man and a woman, a couple, are arguing and it is clear that they are engaged in a familiar ritual. The front door to their house has been left open and they cannot agree whose turn it is to close it. After heated debate they agree that the first of them to speak will do it. They retire to bed.

1.4 Soon a band of thieves discovers the open door, enters the cottage and starts to remove the couple's belongings. Madeleine, one of the robbers, provides the getaway vehicle. The couple look on with open but silent mouths as chairs are piled onto Madeleine's electric wheelchair and she drives them away.

1.5 As one item after another is removed from the cottage, the assembled pupils watch intently and laugh as the home is progressively dismantled. There is a warm and relaxed atmosphere. It's not a high-pressure performance.

1.6 Finally the couple are lifted out of their bed and the burglars remove it. The husband, unable to contain himself any longer, cries out in horror, 'We've lost everything!', whereupon his wife gleefully responds, 'You spoke first, you have to close the door!' The audience claps loudly in appreciation.

1.7 Some of the pupils now read their poems. In the first batch they have punctuated alternate lines with the word 'move'. The poems are written with varying competence but the teacher encourages them equally, putting an arm round shoulders when extra support is needed to overcome first-performance nerves. Gareth and Darren have written their poem together and perform it in unison:

> Move.
> I'm going to whack that ball.
> Move.
> I'm going to bowl that ball.
> Move.
> I'm going to crash that ball.

Move.
I'm going to hit them stumps.
Move.
I'm going to catch that ball.
Move.
Oh no you're not.
Move.

1.8   Madeleine has produced a poem on a light-talker. She cannot talk but can communicate through her computer operated with a knee switch. A voice synthesizer presents her poem with a clipped American voice:

Move.
Look out I'm coming.
Move.
I'm coming fast.
Move.
I will run you over.
Move.

1.9   Gary then steps forward beside Madeleine and rereads the poem for those who did not catch the limited amplification of the voice synthesizer. When the poems have been read and the pupils have applauded once more, the headteacher thanks the class, makes announcements and the pupils disperse for their lessons.

1.10   This glimpse of school life hints at an approach that can be taken to develop the diverse talents of a class group. Using a common starting point or a shared experience each student can be supported to learn and express themselves in a way matched to their attainments and interests. But it is possible that my choice of setting for the assembly made some of you feel less than at home. It was a primary example and you may have greater experience of secondary or special schools or further education, as a parent or a teacher or a student. You may be neither parent nor teacher and you may be hoping that this course doesn't get too involved in the minutiae of curricula. We will try to bear you all in mind.

1.11   Although many of you will be studying in relative isolation, I picture you as a diverse community and it is as well for you to be aware of this diversity. Besides differences of job and experience of education we recognize that you may be based anywhere in the United Kingdom. You may live in an inner city or a rural area; in Northern Ireland or Wales or Scotland or England; in Belfast, Pontypool, Dunfermline or Littleport. We will try to represent the experience of as many of you as possible. You will have to be prepared to learn from experiences which are different from your own.

Learning for all

1.12   The course is concerned with the education of students who experience difficulties or have disabilities and the way schools and curricula can contribute to the prevention, creation or resolution of difficulties. Some of those children and young people are seen, by themselves or by others, as failing in education and some rebel noisily or silently by becoming 'disaffected' or truanting. Among those with disabilities, we include people who are deaf or have visual or physical disabilities. Like Madeleine, they may be helped by technology to gain access to a full range of subjects or they may have limited powers of communication. We are concerned with understanding and preventing difficulties in learning among school students whatever their level of attainment. Only a small proportion of the students with whom we are concerned are formally categorized as 'having learning difficulties' by being the subject of 'statements' (England and Wales) or 'records' (Scotland).

1.13   The course ranges from pre-school to further and higher education. Most of the course, however, deals with the compulsory school years. Unit 5 examines pre-school and Unit 13 is about post-16 education and training.

1.14   However, we are also interested in exploring the extent to which an attempt to make schools responsive to the difficulties in learning or disabilities of *some* students can help to improve the education of *all* students. The title of this unit, *Making Connections,* is a challenge to link the reduction of difficulties in learning to the development of an education system that is responsive to all learners irrespective of their gender, skin colour, ethnicity, background, level of attainment, abilities or disabilities. The course also requires you to draw on your own experience and connect this to your understanding of other people's experience of learning or teaching.

1.15   The practices in such a responsive system were set out in a series of books called *Curricula for All* with the subtitles: *Preventing Difficulties in Learning* (Booth, Potts and Swann, 1987), *Producing and Reducing Disaffection* (Booth and Coulby, 1987) and *Including Pupils with Disabilities* (Booth and Swann, 1987). You may find the two readers for the course E829 *Developing Inclusive Curricula: equality and diversity in education* particularly useful. They have the general title *Equality and Diversity in Education* and the subtitles: *Learning, Teaching and Managing in Schools* (Potts, Armstrong and Masterton, 1995a), and *National and International Contexts* (Potts, Armstrong and Masterton, 1995b).

1.16   'The process of increasing the participation of students in the curriculum and social life of mainstream schools' is one definition of *integration* or *inclusion* in education. This course considers ways to maximize inclusion by removing barriers to learning. It is concerned equally with identifying and minimizing the pressures to exclude students from full participation in the mainstream. The process of exclusion from the mainstream – according to disability or low attainment, or difficulties over student behaviour – sometimes results in a student attending a special school. We will look at policies and practices that minimize such placements. Some of you, including some who work in special schools, may feel that your students are part of this minimum group; students who could not and should not participate in mainstream schools. We hope this course will assist those who work in special schools to enable their students to participate fully within a demanding curriculum which extends their interests and attainments within their schools. We hope, too, that this course will enable all of you to explore the validity of your preconceptions.

Special educational needs

1.17   This course is concerned with learning difficulties, disability and disaffection in education, where disaffection is defined as 'a feeling of dissatisfaction with, opposition to, or rejection of aspects of teaching or learning'. Many of you will think that this means that it is about children and young people with 'special educational needs'. Some of you may have these words in a job title such as 'Special Educational Needs Co-ordinator'. Most of the authors of the units do not use these terms because we think that they are imprecise and interfere with forming our own views about how disabilities, disaffection and difficulties in learning should be understood. However, you will find the term 'children with special needs' used more frequently by authors of the chapters in the readers. Any academic course should challenge received ideas and I think that it is difficult to do so if we repeat their forms of expression.

HOW SHOULD YOU STUDY THIS UNIT?

1.18   This unit contains four main sections after this introduction, and a brief final section providing ideas for your future investigations. Section 2, 'What makes education difficult?', looks at the nature and definition of difficulties in learning, some of the groups of students who face difficulties or devaluation in and out of school, and some of the perspectives from which difficulties are understood. Section 3 explores the question 'How do schools respond to diversity?' through case-studies of the primary school that I used to introduce this unit, and Whitmore comprehensive secondary school. Section 4 is produced as a supplement accompanying the unit; it asks 'How should we react to government policy?' Since this contains the material most likely to date it is produced in supplement form so that we can bring it up to date each year, if necessary. Section 5, 'How should we talk, read and write?', takes up one of the themes of the course, introducing a structure for your approach to critical study.

1.19   The unit represents four weeks of study time. We ask of you what we would aim to achieve with almost any learners; that you take control of your own learning. We expect you to control the amount of time you spend on the course, to be selective where necessary and to look forward or re-examine parts of the course at a later stage, as their significance becomes clear. We have carefully considered the sequence of material so that sections build on each other but you will be the best judge of your particular learning needs.

1.20   Below, I have set out the material additional to this text that will be studied in each section of the unit, and where it can be found.

Section 2 What makes education difficult?

Reader 1, Chapter 22: 'Stressing education: children in care' by Felicity Fletcher-Campbell.

Reader 1, Chapter 24: 'Affected by HIV and AIDS: cameos of children and young people' by Philippa Russell, with an introduction by Tony Booth.

Reader 1, Chapter 23: 'Adolescents, sex and injecting drug use: risks for HIV infection' by Marina Barnard and Neil McKeganey.

Reader 1, Chapter 11: 'In the driving seat? Supporting the education of traveller children' by Chris Mills.

Appendix 1 in this unit: 'Who's to blame? A multi-layered epic' by Dennis Mongon and Susan Hart.

Section 3 How should schools respond to diversity?

TV1 *Under the Walnut Tree*.

Reader 2, Chapter 1: 'Under the walnut tree: the Grove Primary School' by Tony Booth.

Appendix 2 in this unit: 'The open-air school: sunshine, rest and food'.

Reader 1, Chapter 12: 'Chris Raine's progress: an achievement to be proud of' by Alyson Clare.

Reader 2, Chapter 2: 'A curricular response to diversity at Whitmore High School' by Christine Gilbert and Michael Hart.

Section 4 How should we react to government policies?

This is a supplement to be read at this point in the unit. The supplement includes material that covers current government policies – it is supplied in this form to ensure the material can be easily updated as policies change and evolve.

Section 5 How should we speak, write and read?

Reader 1, Chapter 31: '*Le mot juste*: learning the language of equality' by Caroline Roaf.

Reader 1, Chapter 32: 'Writing clearly: contributing to the ideal comprehensibility situation' by Margaret Peter.

2 WHAT MAKES EDUCATION DIFFICULT?

2.1   If you asked school students and teachers to identify the sources of their major difficulties in school you would get different sets of answers. You might get some surprises too. When asked to identify the major difficulty at their school, one group of teachers immediately referred to the school caretaker's policy of controlling access to the toilets and toilet paper. At another school a major dispute centred around the contents of a break-time snack. Bananas were banned from the classroom and the parents of a boy whose favourite food was bananas withdrew him from the school rather than submit to the rule of the carrot and apple (*Cambridge Evening News*, 17 September 1990).

2.2   You might find that students frequently identify the difficulties they have with other students and that teachers have considerable problems with other teachers. Bullying might be uppermost in the minds of many students (Sharp and Smith, 1994; Smith and Sharp, 1994). We are devoting a section of Unit 11/12 to the issue as well as Television Programme 5, *Danger, Children at Play.* No forms of bullying are pleasant but sexual and racial harassment and violence represent particularly insidious forms. Nor is all bullying between students. Students can bully teachers, teachers can bully students and each other. Reprinted below is one teacher's experience of being mercilessly bullied by the headteacher of her school.

Beaten by a head

IKNEW I was a good teacher and I always got on well with my pupils. There were never any discipline problems and I was proud of the fact that I didn't have to refer to the head all the time.

Then one morning, three months after a new head arrived, he walked into my class and demanded to know why I wasn't dictating notes. In front of everyone he said my teaching method was ridiculous.

The next day, when I caught him listening outside the door, he marched in and complained that I'd parked my car in the wrong slot, that I seemed to be incapable of doing anything right.

I remember the anger rising in my chest and colour flooding into my face, but I didn't want to have a shouting match in front of the whole class, so I just kept quiet.

One Monday morning he told me that he no longer had a class for me. Instead, I had to teach different groups, which meant there wasn't the same opportunity to build up a relationship with the pupils. It then became more difficult to keep control because I was always moving about.

Because I felt stateless not having a proper base, a male colleague offered me a working space in his classroom. The head went out of his way to get me removed and he kept calling my colleague into his office to convince himself that we were having an affair.

By that time the atmosphere in the staffroom was appalling. He would always have his knife into one person at a time, apart from those who sided with him to stay out of trouble.

It eventually reached the point where people didn't talk to the person whose turn it was to be bullied, in case they were seen by the head and became the target for further recriminations.

He went on endlessly putting people down and bombarding them with insults, screaming at staff during slanging matches in the corridors. What had once been a school with a lovely atmosphere deteriorated to the extent that the pupils were getting upset and parents weren't wanting to send their children there any more. The union advised us to unite and stand up against him together, but we were so divided by this time and so governed by fear it was unthinkable.

(*Guardian*, 19 June 1990, p. 25)

2.3   But teachers do have particular preoccupations of their own. They are paid to teach and to teach successfully they have to create order. Some see this order as coming from a planned and interesting curriculum while others view the maintenance of order as a separate skill of classroom management passed on from experienced staff to new recruits in tricks of the trade. I will return to matters of control in Unit 11/12.

2.4   This section is not primarily concerned with staff relationships and the need for school order; here I will concentrate on the educational difficulties of *students*. I will start by asking how 'difficulties in learning' should be defined. I suggest that difficulties in learning can best be understood as a breakdown in the relationship between a learner, the curriculum, teachers and other resources that support learning. I then consider some of the ways that learning can be made more difficult, either because students have troubled lives or because their identities, backgrounds or lifestyles are devalued. I will suggest that the way students are valued is an important part of the learning process and that troubled or devalued students may become disaffected or experience difficulties with learning. I will end the section by examining teacher and student perspectives on an incident of student 'disruption'. It illustrates some of the pressures of school life which shape decisions about teaching and learning.

DEFINING DIFFICULTIES IN LEARNING FOR YOURSELF

2.5   For some people the words 'learning difficulties' trigger off a narrow response. They see them as applying to a small group of people, perhaps most commonly to a group of students in schools. Below, I have provided a couple of activities to help in examining such assumptions.

Activity 1   When and why is learning difficult?

Spend a few minutes jotting down responses to the following. Try to recall three occasions when you experienced difficulties in learning something.

- What were you trying to learn?

- What made learning difficult?

- What would have helped you overcome your difficulties?

Activity 2   Making sense of science

In 1985 Robert Hull published a book, *The Language Gap*, about the difficulties experienced by students with the words used in their lessons. Below, I have included an extract from a science lesson that he transcribed. As you read it consider the following:

- What makes learning difficult in this lesson?

- How could the difficulties in learning be overcome?

Particular difficulties

TEACHER: We're going to start today doing radioactivity. (This was announced amidst noise and talk.)

PUPIL 1: Have you got my book, sir?

PUPIL 2: What's the date?

PUPIL 3: Have you got my book, sir?

> And there were other questions as the teacher wrote on the board: 'Introduction – radioactivity'.

PUPIL 4: Is radioactivity all one word? (It was evidently to be a note-dictating session.)

TEACHER: Now I'm going to start by talking a minute about the atom.

PUPIL 5: Radioactivity's hyphenated.

PUPIL 2: S'not!

TEACHER: Now, who knows anything about the atom?

PUPIL 6: Molecule. (Indistinct; the only reply.)

TEACHER: Who knows anything about the structure of the atom? (No reply.)

TEACHER: No? (Pause.) Well, an atom is made up of a nucleus with a positive charge, and around it it has a field of negative charge ... the nucleus is very small ... you could compare it with the size of a pea on the centre spot of Wembley Stadium ... So an atom is mostly ... ? (Pause.) What's in between?

PUPIL 7: Air.

TEACHER: Air is made up of atoms ... What's in [indistinct]?

PUPIL 5: How do you split them?

TEACHER: We're interested in ...

PUPIL 5: How did they find out about the nucleus and [indistinct]?

TEACHER: It would take too long to tell ... it would take half a term in the sixth form. (Noise.) All right, then ... there was this chap called Rutherford ... he produced a sheet of atoms of [indistinct].

PUPIL 5: How?

TEACHER: ... and bombarded it with particles.

PUPIL 5: *Where* did he [bombard them?]

TEACHER: Well, it would take a long time.

ALL PUPILS: Half a term in the sixth form! (Small chorus.)

> Some of what was said in this discussion was indistinct, but the dramatic shape of the passage, the urgency of the questions, and the continuous, rather grudging, redefinition of content as it reflects the teacher's priorities (in particular his need to cope), seem clear.

PUPIL 2: How did he get the atoms off it?

TEACHER: He knocked them …

PUPIL 2: (interrupting) *HOW?!!* How did he get them …

TEACHER: Well …

PUPIL 2: I want to KNOW! (Voice rising in exasperation.)

TEACHER: Jane!

> After this small explosion his exposition went on for a short while uninterrupted by questions, or anything else.

TEACHER: They thought an atom was just solid, but because … [indistinct] they found that 99 per cent went straight through, 0.9 per cent got deflected, but 0.1 per cent got bounced straight back.

PUPILS TOGETHER: Cor!

TEACHER: They couldn't explain it … they thought the only reason could be … the mass was concentrated at one particular point … if all the rest went through [indistinct] … RIGHT, so we have …

PUPIL 8: (interrupting) Is that splitting the atom?

TEACHER: No, we'll get on to that later.

> The teacher then rather abruptly started his dictation of notes.

TEACHER: … small heavy particle, positively charged. It was found that if you shot particles at a nucleus, it would break up. It was found that there were two types of particles, neutrons and protons …

PUPIL 8: So the nucleus [indistinct]?

TEACHER: Well, yes, we'll see …

> The note-taking was completed two minutes or so later with the words: 'surrounding this are electrons in constant motion'. Immediately, a pupil spoke:

PUPIL 9: Do they go round?

TEACHER: Yes, but it's not as simple as that, because they behave both as particles and as waves – it's a very complex part of chemistry.

ALL PUPILS: Half a term in the sixth form? (Small chorus.)

PUPIL 5: University.

(Hull, 1985, p. 121–3)

2.6 The whole science class must have experienced difficulties in learning about radioactivity in this lesson. The teacher does not have a grasp of what students already know, nor that this might differ for each student, nor a clear idea of the best sequence of instruction. There is disorder in the teaching and among the students. Since we are willing to say that these students *experience difficulties in learning* we could also say that they *have learning difficulties*. But the simple rephrasing does not imply that there is something special about the students; in experiencing difficulties in learning, or having learning difficulties, they are just like you or me.

Activity 3   How should learning difficulties be defined?

Think about the way you responded to the last two activities. Sum up your responses by completing the following sentences:

- I have difficulties in learning when …

- The students in the science lesson had difficulties in learning because …

Then write down your considered definition of difficulties in learning:

- A difficulty in learning arises when …

2.7   You may have come up with two sorts of reason for difficulties in learning: those that describe characteristics of a learner, task or teacher, and those that refer to relationships between these. You may have difficulties because you are tired or unable to concentrate because of distracting emotions, or because the task was inappropriate or the teaching uninspiring.

2.8   But we can also think of learning as taking place in relationships between learners, tasks, teachers and resources. *Difficulties in learning arise, then, when there is a mismatch between learners, tasks and teachers.* They arise from a breakdown in these relationships, and can arise for any learner. We can ask whether the teaching and curriculum connect appropriately with the background and experience of any learner, moving their learning forward in a way that values their identity. If we understand difficulties in this way then we can see that a school can draw together its policies on combating sexism, racism and difficulties in learning or providing support for bilingual students.

2.9   This is the approach to defining learning difficulties that I find most helpful. In planning and improving teaching, analysing difficulties in learning or assessing students, it is essential to bear these learning relationships in mind. It seems to me, for example, that if anyone wants to improve the learning of students, to raise standards in education, then it makes little sense to do this by assessing only students, who are just one element of learning relationships. Good teaching involves the continual assessment of the relationship between student and the resources available to support learning.

2.10   By describing difficulties in learning as a mismatch between learners, tasks and teachers, this does not mean that the task of teaching is simply to monitor and control the match between students and tasks. For, as I suggested in the introduction to this unit, education should ultimately aim to enable learners to contribute to the learning process themselves, to select and adjust the nature of the learning tasks so that they are appropriate.

2.11   But because learning difficulties were defined officially in law, in the 1981 Education Act and then in Part III of the 1993 Education Act which replaced it, it is easy to put aside what we know already about our own learning and the learning of others and slip into the official groove (DES, 1981; DFE, 1993). We may feel obliged to do this because we feel deferential to the authority of the words of an Act of Parliament. I think that the sense and value of official definitions is worth examining in some detail so that we can decide for ourselves when and how to use them.

2.12   Section 156 of the 1993 Education Act sets out and inter-relates definitions of 'special educational needs', 'learning difficulties' and 'special educational provision' in the following way (which incidentally makes no concession to conventions of non-sexist English):

1   For the purposes of the Education Acts, a child has 'special educational needs' if he has a learning difficulty which calls for special educational provision to be made for him.

2   For the purposes of this Act, subject to subsection (3) below, a child has a 'learning difficulty' if –

(a)   he has a significantly greater difficulty in learning than the majority of children of his age,

(b)   he has a disability which either prevents or hinders him from making use of educational facilities of a kind generally provided for children of his age in schools within the area of the local education authority, or

(c)   he is under the age of five years and is, or would be if special educational provision were not made for him, likely to fall within paragraph (a) or (b) when over that age.

3   A child is not to be taken as having a learning difficulty solely because the language (or form of the language) in which he is, or will be, taught is different from a language (or form of a language) which has at any time been spoken in his home.

4   In the Education Acts, 'special educational provision' means –

(a)   in relation to a child who has attained the age of two years, educational provision which is additional to, or otherwise different from, the educational provision made generally for children of his age in schools maintained by the local education authority (other than special schools) or grant-maintained schools in their area, and

(b)   in relation to a child under that age, educational provision of any kind.

5   In this Part of this Act, 'child' includes any person who has not attained the age of nineteen years and is a registered pupil at a school.

(Educational Act 1993, Part III, Section 156)

Activity 4   Analysing the definitions in the 1993 Education Act ———

Look at the definitions from the 1993 Act given above and answer the following questions.

1   According to the definitions, what proportion of the school population have learning difficulties?

2   Can a student have learning difficulties on some tasks but not others?

3   Is the number of students who have 'special educational needs' greater than, fewer than or the same as the number of students who have 'learning difficulties'?

4   Would the same children have 'learning difficulties' or 'special educational needs' in different situations?

5   Which children with disabilities have learning difficulties?

6   Would the same children with disabilities have learning difficulties in different situations?

7   Does the proportion of students for whom special educational provision is made depend on the way students are taught routinely?

8   Why are children who have English as an additional language and experience difficulties in learning in school excluded from the official definition of 'learning difficulties' and 'special educational needs'?

———————————————————————————————

The official proportion of students with learning difficulties

2.13   The number of students said to have learning difficulties according to the definition depends on the assumptions we make. If we think of a learning difficulty as a general and persistent characteristic of individuals then the number who could have significantly greater difficulties in learning than the majority would be something less than 50 per cent. Precisely how much less would depend on what meaning we give to 'significantly greater than'. However, if a learning difficulty depends on the task or subject learnt then the number could be higher than 50 per cent since different students find different things difficult. If we drop the notion of persistence, then at some time all students might find some tasks more difficult than the majority, due, for example, to their emotional state.

The official proportion of students with 'special educational needs'

2.14 Presumably the numbers of students said to have 'special educational needs' must be smaller than those said to have 'learning difficulties', since they are a subgroup which 'calls for special educational provision to be made'. However, I suspect that many people use the terms 'special educational needs' and 'learning difficulty' interchangeably.

2.15 A tradition has grown up, attributed to the Warnock Report (DES, 1978), that there are 20 per cent of the school population with special needs. In fact the suggestion in the report was that 'about 1 in 6' (around 17 per cent) of the school population would have 'special educational needs' at any one time with 'up to 20 per cent' having them at some time in their school career (DES, 1978, para. 3.17). But the Warnock Report itself relied on earlier studies of prevalence rates, in which difficulties were defined in terms of a statistical difference from a mean or average. In such circumstances the number of pupils who are said to have difficulties is a *statistical invention* rather than a discovery.

2.16 It has also been argued that the identification of a fixed, large number of students with special needs is in the interests of those who work in the special education system and who wish to mark out a sizeable territory as their sphere of influence. Others have offered further reasons for discovering large numbers of pupils with special needs. The learning difficulties of pupils can absolve schools from the responsibility for failing to teach them. Further, in an economy with rising unemployment, it may be useful for governments to identify a large section of the population whose deficiencies are thought to make it difficult for them to cope with paid work.

2.17 One way to exhibit the dependence of difficulties on the nature of curricula and teaching is to regard 'special educational needs' as 'unmet needs'. However, while this may clarify the term 'special', it does not avoid the problems with the word 'need'. I need food, but I may also be said to need 'taking down a peg or two' or a child may be said to need 'a good hiding' – an assertion that says more about the wishes and satisfactions of its producer than its beneficiary. The 'needs' in 'special needs' are not biological like hunger nor uncontentiously satisfied as by providing food. When 'professionals' talk of the identification of special needs, they obscure their part in defining what is in a child's best interests.

'Learning difficulties', 'special needs' and circumstances

2.18 If placing a figure on the number of pupils who have 'special educational needs' is essentially arbitrary, why do people do it? I think it is a consequence of applying a medical analogy with disease, to educational difficulties. Children are thought to 'have learning difficulties' like an illness which is more or less incurable. In the case of a disease, it makes sense to ask whether someone has it or not. Yet, even according to the official definitions, the numbers of students experiencing learning difficulties will depend on how well teachers are resourced and able to respond to a diversity of learners.

Disability and learning difficulty

2.19 According to the definitions some children who have disabilities have learning difficulties. But these are not related either to a general lack of proficiency *or* to a difficulty over particular tasks. It is assumed, instead, that it is the disabilities some children have which 'prevent or hinder' their participation in the mainstream. Consider a child in a wheelchair in an area where schools generally have doorways too narrow to permit wheelchair access, or where there are steps with no ramps, or more than one storey but no lift. Or consider another child, a deaf sign language user. In these circumstances, what is it that 'prevents or hinders' the participation of students? You or I might argue that it is the size of doorway or absence of ramps or lifts or of sign language support. However, in applying the Act the definition is routinely taken to mean that the child in a wheelchair, rather than the school or local authority, has a learning difficulty.

2.20 The discriminatory nature of this definition was pointed out forcefully during the committee stage of the Education Bill, before it was enshrined in the 1993 Education Act:

> Under the law ... my constituent Stephen Hawking has a learning difficulty. That is a good example which shows how absurd the definitions are. ... The failure to provide lifts or accessible doorways and toilets prevents disabled teachers and support staff as well as disabled parents, grandparents or other members of the community from entering schools. ... The onus should be on the buildings, not the [disabled] person.
>
> (Anne Campbell, MP, 1993, *Parliamentary Debates: Education Bill*, 1059–1060)

It seemed astonishing that the same lack of sensitivity or critical thought which led to the inclusion of this definition in the 1981 Education Act should lead to its repetition over a decade later. This is, perhaps, one measure of the lack of progress in thinking in the Department for Education.

2.21 In later units, you will return to an examination of the meaning of 'disability'. It will be argued that what disables a person with an impairment are the excluding practices of society which often take all too concrete forms.

Special educational provision

2.22 Presumably special educational provision is to be contrasted with ordinary educational provision. If schools are staffed and resourced so that they routinely cater for the diversity of their pupils, then fewer students require 'special educational provision'.

A BRIEF HISTORY OF TERMS

Education Act 1981:

A child has a learning difficulty if he has a disability which prevents or hinders …

Education Act 1993:

A child has a learning difficulty if he has a disability which prevents or hinders …

The theoretical physicist and best-selling author of
A Brief History of Time, Stephen Hawking, is a
wheelchair user who communicates (like Madeleine)
with a light talker.

Learning difficulty and language

2.23   The position of students who learn English as an additional language, since a different language is spoken at home, closely parallels that of many students with disabilities. They might have a difficulty with the curriculum because it is not accessible to them, and to contribute effectively they need support. However, any difficulties in learning experienced by students because they speak English as an additional language, are not officially to be called 'learning difficulties'.

2.24   I think this muddle in definitions arises because of a strong tradition in education which attributes the difficulties students have with learning to something deficient in the students themselves. The first two official definitions could be replaced by the following, with little effect on the way they are used in practice:

> a child has a learning difficulty when he or she has a deficiency which makes learning more difficult than for the majority of students of his or her age.

2.25   Saying that a child has a 'learning difficulty' or special needs or a disability is not just a neutral description which helps to enable an appropriate education to be provided for them. It also confers a label which carries negative connotations of mental or physical imperfection. But if we should avoid negatively labelling pupils whose first language is not English, shouldn't we do this for all pupils?

Subjects of formal assessment

2.26   Within the definitions of the 1993 Act there is a progressive narrowing down from students who have learning difficulties, to students with 'special educational needs'. This process is continued both in the definition of those who should have formal assessments and in defining who should be the subject of a legally binding summary record and educational prescription, known as a Statement of Special Educational Needs in England and Wales and a Record in Scotland. I shall have more to say about this process in Section 4 of this unit, 'How should we react to government policies?'.

2.27   According to the 1993 Act a child should be the subject of a formal assessment if he or she 'falls, or probably falls' within a group defined by the following:

(a)   he has special educational needs, and

(b)   it is necessary for the authority to determine the special educational provision which any learning difficulty he may have calls for.

(Education Act 1993, Part III, Clause 167)

2.28   There is no way in which we could determine the size of this group simply by looking at these definitions. Statements are to be written for those students for whom it is definitely deemed necessary by the authority that they should 'determine' the provision. The government has issued guidance that statements should be provided for around 2 per cent of the school population (DFE, 1994). Working back from this official estimation of numbers we can see that the subjects of formal assessments are meant to be somewhat, but not too much, greater than this. I leave you to puzzle over how often an outcome has to occur in order for it to be 'probably' about to happen.

2.29   The figure of 2 per cent as the number of students officially expected to be the subject of statements has been handed down from the numbers often said to 'require' an education in special schools (DES, 1978). This is an overestimate by 50 per cent of the numbers currently educated within such schools. But the coincidence of numbers gives some indication of where many people expect the majority of students with statements to be educated.

Definitions of learning difficulty in the 1994 Code of Practice

2.30   If you need further reason for working with your own definition of difficulty in learning rather than the official ones, then it is provided by the 1994 Code of Practice (DFE, 1994). This gives guidance on the interpretation of the 1993 Act. In addition to the learning difficulties of the Act, it suggests the following types of learning difficulty (see DFE, 1994, Section 3):

learning difficulty;

specific learning difficulty or dyslexia;

emotional and behavioural difficulty;

physical disability;

hearing difficulty;

visual difficulty;

speech and language difficulty;

medical conditions.

2.31   Yes, it really does suggest that a 'learning difficulty' is a type of 'learning difficulty'. The confusion occurs because it uses the term in different ways without any recognition that this has taken place. The Code of Practice introduces a definition of 'learning difficulty' to refer explicitly to students who are *relatively low in attainment* compared to others of their age as one type of the broader 1993 Act 'learning difficulties'. I will return to this issue in Section 4's supplement.

Flying Crooked

The butterfly, a cabbage-white,
(His honest idiocy of flight)
Will never now, it is too late,
Master the art of flying straight,
Yet has – who knows so well as I? –
A just sense of how not to fly:
He lurches here and here by guess
And God and hope and hopelessness.
Even the aerobatic swift
Has not his flying-crooked gift.

(Robert Graves, in Kavanagh and Michie, 1985, p. 216)

2.32   While, on my definition, all students experience difficulties in
learning at some time, it is clear that, at any one time, some students are
more likely to experience difficulties than others. If we have a narrow
notion of an ideal student and create education around that ideal, then
others are likely to encounter difficulties. The official definitions of
learning difficulty *imply* that students with relatively low attainments will
experience difficulties, and suggest more directly that students with
disabilities and those who learn English as an additional language will
find education problematic too.

2.33   Students with particular talents, who may include disabled
students, bilingual students, or students who have low attainments in
some areas but not others, are also likely to find that they pose a
challenge and thereby experience difficulties in learning in many schools.
One might argue that defining 'learning difficulties' in terms of
differences from a 'norm' of performance or appearance is actually one of
the causes of difficulties in learning. Such an argument may be more
readily acknowledged outside school. The problems caused by the
tyrannies of masculine or feminine 'normality' are frequently aired. As
inside schools, the 'normal' and the 'ideal' become confused and the
search for normality controls and eludes us. In reality it is normal to be
different.

2.34   The idea that there is a typical student can easily invade our
images of difference. Thus we may picture a child in a wheelchair as
typically disabled, and the exclusion from school on disciplinary grounds
as typically the result of a violent confrontation with teachers, even
though such violence is rarely involved (see Unit 11/12). We have to
learn to use our typical images as metaphors; standing for all the ways in
which students can differ one from the other.

2.35   In what follows, I have attempted to draw attention to a small
number of ways in which the background, experiences and
preoccupations of students may be implicated in the difficulties that they

experience in schools. In some cases, the difficulties may be emotional initially, but it requires a particular talent to prevent emotional difficulties interfering with learning. Where the emotional pressure is a direct result of the 'tyranny of normality', schools can do much to alleviate it, at source.

2.36 I have highlighted a few issues because I see them as pertinent and instructive, but you will be aware that there are other ways of grouping students so that they become a focus of our concern. Sometimes, problems which have been given relatively little consideration become a focus of concern for some teachers because of the level of media attention they receive. In the late 1980s and early 1990s a number of cases of child sexual abuse achieved notoriety in the press in Cleveland, Rochdale, Nottingham, Kent and elsewhere. Mica Nava has written an account of the media attention given to the Cleveland child sexual abuse cases which I found helpful in thinking out my own reactions (Nava, 1988; see also Doyle, 1989, and Maher, 1987). Whatever the merits of particular allegations, there is no escaping the fact that child sexual abuse is uncomfortably widespread. However, the separation of child abuse into cases of sexual and non-sexual abuse may deflect attention from the far greater number of children who suffer from the latter.

Children in care

2.37 Children in care form one of the most vulnerable groups in society and education. There are continuing concerns about the lack of support they receive over education and which can amount to informal exclusion from school (Social Services Inspectorate/Office for Standards in Education, 1995; Stirling, 1992). They are a relatively small group. At 66,000, they are about half the size of the group currently in special schools. The great majority are in foster homes. Media attention has been focused on the remaining group in children's homes because of the high profile given to investigations of child sexual abuse and abuses of power by the 'carers' in social services departments.

Activity 5   A concern for education

While we were preparing this course we were contacted by Felicity Fletcher-Campbell of the National Foundation for Educational Research because she was concerned that we might omit a discussion of the educational vulnerability of children in care. We asked her to write a short chapter setting out her thoughts on the education of children in care; we have included this as Chapter 22 in Reader 1. As you read the chapter, consider a list of questions you would wish to ask to find out whether a group of six young people in a small children's home were being educated appropriately. Whom would you wish to talk to?

2.38 I would wish to discuss the children's education with teachers, social workers and childcare workers in the children's home as well as the children themselves. The following questions are some of those to which I would hope to obtain answers:

- Who has responsibility for ensuring that the young people receive appropriate education and what steps do they take to fulfil this role?

- Is there good contact between home and school?

- Does a particular person in the children's home make time to discuss the school day, to give support and help with homework?

- Do the teachers and childcare workers respect the ordinary rights of the young people to privacy?

- What steps are taken to maximize educational continuity?

- What steps are taken to encourage the young people, their teachers and careworkers to have high expectations for educational attainment?

2.39   A list of questions such as this can make the issues seem simplistic. Like anyone else, a young person in care has complex needs for emotional support and encouragement, and an intelligent recognition and assessment of the best way for them to progress in education. Felicity Fletcher-Campbell argues that because young people in care have other pressing needs their education may be overlooked. However, it is clear from the testimony of young people and from reports on their care that their basic human rights may be overlooked too, and that this may make it a far from simple matter to increase attention on their education.

Pinning down the problems in care

2.40   In 1979, Barbara Kahan published a book called *Growing up in Care* which was based on taped discussions between ten adults about their experiences in care between 1942 and 1969 (Kahan, 1979). The group identified the same problems in education as those identified by Felicity Fletcher-Campbell:

> They recognized very clearly that their attitude to school had been related to where they were living and whether the adults caring for them were concerned about their educational progress. Barry described how when he was in a children's home he was fifth from the bottom of the class of over forty, but when he was boarded out his class results got better each term until he was third from the top. He could not explain why this had happened except that his foster mother and an older boy in the family had both taken an interest in his progress and encouraged him in a variety of ways, some direct, others indirect.
>
> (Kahan, 1979, p. 150)

2.41   In 1991 Barbara Kahan was co-author of a report into childcare practices in Staffordshire (Kahan and Levy, 1991). This centred on an investigation into 'pin down', a system of control involving solitary confinement practised in four of the county's children's homes between 1983 and 1989.

> In the most extreme form of pin down, youngsters were deprived of all possessions and clothing except underwear, nightwear and dressing gowns; they were required to stay in a bedroom night and day, knocking on the door for permission to go the toilet; they were deprived of all contact with other residents, refused magazines, music, television, cigarettes or telephone calls; they were denied education and, sometimes, any reading or writing materials; and they were required to get up at 7.00 am and go to bed at 7.00 pm after a bath.
>
> At least 132 youngsters, a figure the report describes as probably conservative, were subjected to the regime. Of these, 81 were boys and 51 girls. One was kept in continuous pin down for 84 days; another was put in twelve times when aged between eleven and fourteen; two others, one boy and one girl, were put in when they were nine.
>
> (*Guardian*, 31 May 1991, p. 2)

2.42 One of the most disturbing features of the report is that the regime appeared to be widely known among staff within Staffordshire Social Services and its practices were openly logged. As one entry remarked: 'Another week of solitary confinement for X has had some rather peculiar effects. He is talking to himself a great deal and we have had tears several times during the course of the week' (*Guardian*, 31 May 1991, p. 2).

2.43 Following the report, the problems of children in care were highlighted in the media for a while. It was argued that with the increase in fostering many of the children who remained in care were those who had problems which made them difficult to look after:

> Ironically, some might say scandalously, these most 'challenging' young people are often in the care of the least experienced and most poorly-trained social workers.
>
> Because they are in a declining sector of social work, residential children's homes find it difficult to retain trained staff. As homes close, opportunities for promotion disappear and staff often leave after qualification for better prospects. Only one in five of those working in residential children's homes have a social work qualification. Their wages and conditions are significantly worse than those in field social work.
>
> (*Times Educational Supplement*, 7 June 1991, p. 6)

2.44 These problems of staffing have been apparent for decades yet little is done to provide appropriate rewards and training for one of the most difficult and responsible jobs within social services.

2.45 Some of the children and young people in care attend boarding schools for students categorized as having emotional and behavioural difficulties, like Wilburton Manor mentioned later in this unit and looked at in greater detail in Unit 11/12. Even these young people cannot be guaranteed respect. The head of one private boarding special school, Castle Hill in Shropshire, was jailed for twelve years for sexually abusing eight of his pupils (*Times Educational Supplement*, 7 June 1991, p. 8).

2.46   The danger of pupils in boarding schools being subjected to sexual abuse was recognized with the setting up of a helpline for pupils at risk. The irony of such abuses is that sexual abuse by parents is a major reason for children being taken into care. This is a route to care that Felicity Fletcher-Campbell fails to mention. Yet, as the *Observer* reported:

> Nottingham Social Services Department discovered that 48 of the 380 children in its residential homes had been sexually abused.

> Most were in care because of sexual abuse, but they were found to be suffering further abuse from other residents. Six young people were said to have been abused for the first time by other children in the homes.

> (*Observer*, 2 June 1991, p. 4)

2.47   The findings in Nottingham were said by the Director of Social Services there to be symptomatic of 'a crisis in residential care ... it is increasingly difficult to control the behaviour of children in care all of the time. The daily demands of working in this sector stretch even the most skilled and experienced staff' (*Observer*, 2 June 1991, p. 4). The Director of Oxfordshire Social Services, however, argued that ordinarily practice was good: 'Let me make a plea for the vast majority of homes that don't run penal regimes, don't beat children and offer lots of love and affection' (*Observer*, 2 June 1991, p. 4).

2.48   What are the problems of children in care? What is provision like in your area? Such questions could form the basis of an investigation later in the course.

The impact of HIV and AIDS

2.49   Children who are HIV positive are progressing through the education system and some will develop AIDS during the course of their education. Some of those who develop AIDS will die during their school days. Already children who are HIV positive have been the victims of prejudice in schools in the United Kingdom, though no-one has gone to the lengths of a judge in Florida who ordered that a six-year-old child should be kept within a glass bubble within the classroom (*Independent*, 11 August 1988).

2.50   It is difficult to predict the priority that we will need to give in education to children and young people affected by HIV and AIDS in the United Kingdom, but we know that the epidemic is progressing rapidly in some areas within the adult population: 'In Inner London the rates of seropositivity [the presence in the blood of HIV antibodies] among sexually active women are doubling every twelve months; if this rate of increase continues the figures will soon approach those of New York and other United States cities' (*The Lancet*, 1991, p. 1572).

2.51   AIDS is already the leading cause of death among women aged 25 to 40 in New York (Chin, 1990). Government statisticians at the Department of Health are guarded about the trends for children. Nevertheless, apart from those children and young people who are HIV positive themselves, many more live with the stress of having a parent or other relative who has HIV infection or AIDS. There were 581 children aged fourteen or under in the United Kingdom who were known to have been infected with HIV-1 virus up to the end of October 1994. Of these 132 had died.

Activity 6   Affected by HIV and AIDS

Now read Chapter 24 in Reader 1, 'Affected by HIV and AIDS: cameos of children and young people' by Philippa Russell. As you read the chapter consider the impact that HIV and AIDS is likely to have on the support that children may need in school. The situation will change within the life of this course. Your knowledge of up-to-date statistics and educational practices may enable you to use the reading to reflect on the changes that have occurred.

2.52   The incidence of HIV and AIDS in some parts of the world, particularly sub-Saharan Africa, will stretch and swamp adult and child welfare services in the coming years. There are reports of 600,000 children orphaned because their parents have died of AIDS in Zimbabwe alone (*Guardian*, 31 March 1995). Worldwide, 750,000 children are estimated to have AIDS, while the estimate for children with HIV infection is up to ten times this number (WHO, 1994, p. 221). The World Health Organization estimated that by the end of 1994 over 4.5 million cases of AIDS had occurred worldwide; the projected total of cases of HIV infection by the year 2000 is 30–40 million, 90 per cent of whom will be in developing countries (WHO, 1995, p. 98). Since I wrote the introduction to the chapter, more information has become available about the transmission of HIV and the progression from HIV to AIDS that will affect predictions about children with HIV and AIDS in school in the United Kingdom. There is unlikely to be much increase in numbers affected by contaminated blood as blood products are now treated effectively in the UK. Up to the end of 1994, 22,645 people were known to have HIV-1 infection, of whom 10,272 had developed AIDS.

2.53   The transmission rate from mothers to their newborn babies is being revised downwards. According to the European Collaborative Study, only 13 per cent of babies born to mothers who are HIV positive remain HIV positive themselves. All of these babies are born with antibodies to HIV in their blood but most are not infected with the virus (European Collaborative Study, 1991). The authors of this report remain undecided about whether transmission of the virus takes place within the uterus or at delivery.

2.54   A number of studies agree that in the developed world the progression from HIV to AIDS takes place in approximately 50 per cent of people within ten years, though there is variation with age (Lee, 1990). Older people tend to progress from HIV to AIDS more rapidly. Babies may progress very rapidly indeed. 30 per cent of those babies who are infected with the virus develop AIDS within the first six months of life (European Collaborative Study, 1991).

2.55   There is some evidence that some drugs, particularly in combination, retard the onset of AIDS and this has implications for testing policies and speed of intervention particularly with babies. Only one-fifth of the number of mothers discovered to be HIV positive in a London study by testing for antibodies in their newborn babies were known to be HIV positive before testing. Questions can be raised about the ethics of such anonymous testing which did not permit particular individuals to be identified, informed and offered treatment (Ades et al., 1991).

HIV and drug use

2.56   Because HIV infection can be passed on by infected blood, the sharing of needles by injecting drug users is a major way in which the infection has spread in the United Kingdom. The infection is then spread further by sexual partners of injecting drug users with HIV infection. In areas of the country where injecting drug use is high, young people who have unprotected sex are at particular risk. One of the central messages of education about HIV and AIDS is that 'there are no high-risk groups, only high-risk behaviours'. Are young people continuing to put themselves at risk?

Activity 7   Young people at risk?

Now read 'Adolescents, sex and injecting drug use: risks for HIV infection', by Marina Barnard and Neil McKeganey (Reader 1, Chapter 23). The chapter provides graphic illustrations of the circumstances that may lead to hard drug and needle use and hence increase in the risk of HIV infection. As you read the chapter consider the following general and specific issues:

(a) Are you satisfied with the methods for gaining information from the young people and that they yielded accurate information?

(b) What picture do you get of the students' world outside school? What effects might this have on the approach taken towards education by pupils and teachers?

(c) What are the risks for HIV infection of these students? Imagine two scenarios. Think of a girl or boy who starts injecting drugs by sharing a needle. Think of a girl or boy who has unprotected sex with a person with HIV. What circumstances lead to these two young people putting themselves at risk?

2.57   My responses are:

(a)   The authors do not say whether parents of the young people were informed that a research project was taking place within the school. Should their consent have been sought?

(b)   I find the chapter informative and clear. The area is economically poor and the pressures for drug use are high but there is a strong sense of community. It is a setting in which teachers may be tempted to have low expectations for students and where students may have a limited view of the possibilities for their future. These are issues to which I will return in Unit 11/12.

(c)   Some of us may feel reluctant to consider the details of the scenarios I suggested. Embarrassment about sexual intercourse or the use of condoms is not confined to young people, nor, of course, is engaging in risky unprotected sex. To have a realistic chance of understanding and tackling these issues with young people we may have to acknowledge and confront our own feelings and behaviour.

2.58   It is easy to use language about HIV and AIDS that is inaccurate or offends or discriminates against people with HIV or AIDS. The chart in Figure 1 (overleaf) provides some guidelines on terms to use and avoid.

Traveller children

2.59   Traveller children and their families have been and continue to be subjected to prejudice outside and inside schools. More than 250,000 travellers were killed during the Nazi occupation of Europe (Liégeois, 1987). In analysing English books for children published between 1914 and 1984, Dennis Binns suggested that there was no other group 'so constantly maligned and misrepresented' (Binns, 1984). The Criminal Justice and Public Order Act 1994 reduced the requirement of and payment to local authorities to provide sites for travellers; it also gave the police additional powers to prevent travellers camping on or stopping on 'private' land. It appears that it will 'effectively outlaw a whole way of life and erode the human rights' of travellers (Morton, 1994, p. 42).

2.60   The term 'traveller' can encompass a whole variety of groups of people. It includes gypsies, fairground and circus people, new age travellers – in fact anyone who adopts a nomadic lifestyle or has previously adopted one. Kenrick and Bakewell (1990) identify five main culturally distinct groups of gypsies in the UK, of whom Romanies form the largest group (about 50,000 people according to Kenrick and Bakewell). Estimates of total numbers of travellers in the UK varies with the source. An upper figure of 110,000 is given in Liégeois (1987) and the lowest figure of 30,000 by HMI (DES, 1985b).

Terms to avoid	Why?	Use instead
• **Carrying AIDS** • **AIDS carrier** • **AIDS positive**	This confuses the two distinct phases of being infected with HIV and having AIDS. People 'have' AIDS, they don't 'carry' it.	*HIV antibody positiv* *People with HIV*
• **AIDS test**	The most commonly used test detects antibodies to HIV. There cannot be a test for AIDS, as this depends on a diagnosis according to clinical symptoms.	*HIV antibody test*
• **AIDS virus**	Can easily cause confusion between HIV and AIDS unless used with caution.	*HIV (Human Immun deficiency Virus)*
• **Catching AIDS**	It isn't possible to catch AIDS. It is possible to catch HIV, but even this is misleading as it suggests transmission is similar to colds or flu.	*Contract HIV* *Become HIV positiv(*
• **Full blown AIDS**	When the correct distinction between HIV and AIDS is made, there is no need to use the term 'full blown AIDS'.	*AIDS*
• **AIDS sufferer**	Having AIDS doesn't mean being ill all the time. Someone with AIDS may continue to work and live a normal life after diagnosis. 'Sufferer' is therefore inappropriate.	*Person with AIDS*
• **Plague**	Plague suggests a contagious disease, which AIDS is not.	*Epidemic*
• **Innocent victim**	Suggests anyone else with AIDS is guilty.	
• **High risk groups**	It is clear that there is risk behaviour, not risk groups. Classification as a member of any particular group does not put anyone at greater risk.	

Figure 1   Talking about HIV and AIDS (ACTUP (Aids Coalition to Unleash Power), London)

2.61   Dennis Binns has written about the history of travellers' education and has traced the competing attitudes towards them. He records the efforts to have the children of travellers removed from their families at the turn of the century: 'The ranks of the criminal classes are largely recruited from our vagrant population, and it is due to the state that steps should be taken to cut off that source of supply by removing children from a vicious environment' (Adams, 1898; quoted in Binns, 1990, p. 253).

2.62   The Children Act of 1908 gave powers of arrest to the police if there was a suspicion that a school-age child of a traveller was not attending school: 'Any constable who finds a person wandering from place to place and taking a child with him may … apprehend him without a warrant, and may take the child to a place of safety' (Children Act 1908, clause 118). It was recognized that the need for casual farm labour in the summer months might involve people in travelling, but to be exempt from prosecution from April to September a traveller had to have 'obtained a certificate of having made not less than 200 attendances at a public elementary school during the months of October to March immediately preceding' (Children Act 1908, clause 118). Binns quotes an anonymous article which argued against the punitive sentiments in the Children Act 1908 and offered a basis for the education of traveller children: 'Reformers must seek, not to adapt the Gypsies to an imperfect educational system which happens to exist, but to remould that system to fit the manner of the life of the Gypsies' (Binns, 1990, p. 254).

2.63   However, seventy years on, in a study of a secondary school intriguingly entitled *Catch 22 Gypsies* (Ivatts, 1975), the presence of traveller children was seen by many staff as a disruption to school routine: 'Many senior members of staff are of the opinion that the school cannot offer them anything in the present situation. The children "beat the system every time" and "if you give them an inch they take a yard" and in most ways are "out of tone with the school"' (Ivatts, 1975, p. 14). The school was particularly concerned about uniform and teachers appeared affronted that the traveller pupils might not assign it the same value as themselves: 'Another facet of behaviour which identifies the Gypsies as a disruptive and uncooperative group is the persistent failure to wear school uniform … the wearing of jewellery is also against school rules and periodic purges usually hit the Gypsies hard with their liking for precious metal, rings and earrings' (Ivatts, 1975, p. 13). Do teachers and researchers continue to use such stereotypes?

Activity 8   In the driving seat

Now read 'In the driving seat? Supporting the education of traveller children' by Chris Mills (Reader 1, Chapter 11). In it, Chris Mills describes her work as a support teacher, attempting to make schools more responsive to the needs of traveller children and to counteract prejudice towards them. As you read it, try to examine your own feelings towards traveller children and their families. Make a list of the efforts a school community might make to attract the traveller children in its area into school. How would you start?

2.64   You may have a number of imaginative ideas about how to make welcome within a school a group of visitors to an area or longer-term traveller residents of a designated site. Should teachers and students visit travellers in their homes?

2.65   Should the traveller lifestyle visible within the books and curriculum materials of the school?

2.66   There are pressures in the 1980 and 1988 Education Acts for schools to move away from the idea that they serve a particular catchment area. Within these Acts, the ideas of parental choice and open enrolment are an encouragement to schools to seek to attract parents from beyond their immediate areas. However, in many schools teachers continue to see themselves as having responsibility for education in a particular community and they would have to see themselves in this way if they were to be motivated to attract the traveller children in their community.

2.67   The staff would need to agree that traveller children were to be actively encouraged to attend the school and prejudices of staff would need to be aired and overcome. The multicultural adviser or advisory teacher of staff in another school with successful experience of working with traveller children might be recruited to help at this stage.

2.68   The students in the school too would need to be encouraged to be welcoming to new students to the school who might stay for varying periods of time.

Activity 9   What do you see?

Figure 2 is taken from a book called *Darwin for Beginners* (Miller and van Loon, 1982). It was used to help to explain why people fail to see facts that are staring them in the face. Jonathan Miller's argument was that the facts to support a theory of evolution were there to be recognized and interpreted by Darwin and others long before the theory of natural selection was composed. Look at the series of drawings and remarks.

Now look again at the central picture. What does this suggest about attitudes to women, old people and travellers?

What prevents us from seeing prejudice when it is staring us in the face?

Figure 2 (Miller and van Loon, 1982, p. 8).

2.69   Children in care, or who are affected by HIV and AIDS, or from travelling families, may present challenges to schools. Where these or other students are seen as less valued members of the school community than others, this may become a reason for disaffection, and may thereby interfere with learning. The sense that a central aspect of your identity is devalued and unrepresented in the school curriculum may create particular pressures, for example, on the education of gay and lesbian young men and women. In order to support the learning of students we have to become aware of prejudice and attempt to overcome it. We should do it because prejudice or discrimination creates a double injustice. There is the injury it causes initially and the consequences it may have on opportunities for learning.

2.70   Discrimination against people because of their skin colour or gender or class or sexuality or disability or attainment is rife in society and in education. If you are not aware of this, then reading may help you, but the best evidence is out there in the world that you encounter every day. Yet some people find such evidence hard to absorb. Writing in the *Times Educational Supplement*, Anthony Flew takes issue with the idea in the Commission for Racial Equality's (CRE) code of practice, that racism accounts for the over-representation of black students in school exclusion figures:

> The code expresses concern 'over the number of ethnic minority pupils being suspended, particularly those of Afro-Caribbean origin' and reports findings that in Birmingham 'black pupils were four times more likely to be suspended than white pupils'. But the CRE never as much as entertains the thought that the true explanation of this disparity may lie in actual differences – differences which are themselves no doubt culturally rather than racially determined – between the behaviour of members of the racial sets thus compared.
>
> (Flew, 1990, p. 23)

2.71   The causes of a student's actions are often complex; they may be part of a 'multi-layered epic' as we shall see in Fred's story below. Yet it seems from this quotation that Flew 'never as much as entertains the thought that' racism may itself contribute to real differences in behaviour as well as to a bias in its interpretation and the reaction to it. The latter processes have been carefully documented by Sally Tomlinson (1981) and Gillborn (1990). The prevalence of racism in education is described in the Swann, Eggleston and Macdonald Reports (DES, 1985a; Eggleston *et al.*, 1985; Macdonald *et al.*, 1989).

2.72   Discrimination against women has been documented in a vast literature in the last twenty years. One of the most visible manifestations of sexism in education is the over-representation of men in positions of power (De Lyon and Widdowson-Migniuolo, 1989; Acker, 1989). Others have documented the sexual harassment of girls as well as the difficulties that teachers have in paying as much attention to girls as to boys in classroom discussion (Jones, 1985; Herbert, 1989; Pye, 1990). In such circumstances it is remarkable that the performance of girls at school in all areas of the curriculum is actually better than that of boys.

2.73   The use of ability to rank pupils is discussed further at the end of the next section. The devaluation of pupils relative to others creates and replenishes a pool of potential disaffection in schools. Whether or not the potential is realized may depend on a number of factors, not least on the efficiency of methods of control.

LOOKING FOR TROUBLE?

2.74   Every conflict in school is part of a complex story. Sometimes processes of devaluation are clearly implicated in the story but at other times this is less clear. You will recall from your own schooldays, if not from your current involvement in schools, that some students find themselves in trouble with remarkable ease, whereas others no less deserving of censure coast along.

Activity 10   Perspectives on trouble

'Who's to blame? A multi-layered epic' by Susan Hart and Dennis Mongon is Appendix 1 in this unit. It is adapted from Chapter 2 of *Improving Classroom Behaviour: new directions for teachers and pupils* (Mongon *et al.*, 1989). In it the authors draw on their experience of secondary teaching to attempt to describe an incident of school life from a variety of points of view of teachers and students. It is a fictionalized account but the competing and clashing views of education which it contains are intended to be authentic.

If you are not a secondary-school teacher, you may find that there are references in this appendix to a world with which you have little acquaintance. As you read it, consider the assumptions that are made about our knowledge of this world. I suggest that you also bear in mind the following questions.

*   Is it desirable and/or possible for teachers in a school to have an agreed approach towards the difficulties encountered by pupils?

*   What power should a specialist teacher in Mary's position have to decide how pupils like Jack and Fred are returned to mainstream lessons?

*   Do some pupils become identified as troublemakers and does this increase the likelihood of their being injured innocents?

*   How can the gender of pupils and teachers affect issues of discipline in a school?

2.75   In secondary schools there may be 'heads of year', 'tutors' and 'tutor groups' who are expected to keep 'journals' up-to-date. There is an emphasis on registers. There may be an 'on-site disruptive unit' in which some staff work for part of their time. Although the unit is on-site, getting to it may involve crossing a muddy field.

2.76   We are also expected to understand something about the practice of suspension or exclusion. Among other issues, the 1986 Education Act dealt with changes in the procedures for exclusion from schools which were further revised in the 1993 Act. It also ended corporal punishment in state, but not private, schools in England and Wales. The word 'suspension' does not figure as a legal term. The head has the right to exclude a pupil for a fixed time or to recommend permanent exclusion but must inform parents immediately and tell them of their right of appeal to the governing body and the LEA who both have powers to reinstate a pupil in a mainstream school, though the LEA has no such power over grant-maintained schools. Governors have a right to appeal against the decision of a local authority who reinstates a pupil against their wishes.

2.77   In Pilgrim's Way there are clear conflicts over the way teachers should respond to pupils like Fred. Teachers can feel that a huge amount of work with a pupil can be undermined as soon as this pupil touches another point in the system. One solution to such conflicts is for a school to attempt to reach an explicit agreement between all staff, as in Whitmore High School described in the following section of this unit. Alternatively a teacher in Mary's position could be given formal responsibility for formulating the approach to be taken. In either case, the agreements can only work with the active co-operation of all the teachers concerned.

2.78   The teachers in the story differ in how they attribute responsibility for producing disruption among the actions of pupils, the behaviour of teachers and the nature of the curriculum. The appendix's authors argue that difficulties can be reduced effectively only through an examination of the way the school is organized, the nature of the curriculum and the manner of its presentation:

> As far as Fred's own 'story' is concerned, Sheila is merely acting out a symbolic role which could potentially have been filled by any representative of the school's authority. Had she acted differently, the incident might have been prevented on this occasion. But it has to be recognized that the likelihood of a confrontation that would provoke Fred's suspension occurring on another occasion would be an ever-present possibility as long as the vicious circle continued to operate, through which Fred, in turn, rejected and was rejected by his school. Our experience suggests that the crisis which occurred on Fred's return to class after a 'successful' period in the unit is typical of what so often happens. A colleague formerly working in an on-site unit for 'disruptive' pupils describes the problem as follows:

It was as though the pupil would come to us for a boost of confidence. We would spend six weeks or so healing the wounds of shattered confidence only to return the pupil to circumstances in which we could predict the scab would be picked and festered in very little time.

Why would pupils who could work hard, behave sensitively and appear to enjoy coming to school when in the unit, behave so differently in the atmosphere of the main school? At least one pupil a year would end up expelled for their behaviour on the main site, despite the work they had put in with the unit. We were failing to prepare them for the 'real world' of school and, in retrospect, too much of our time was spent trying to teach the students strategies which might enable them to foresee or circumvent potentially difficult situations without bringing teaching staff or the pupils' peers into the process. Consequently, the emphasis for blame and remediation lay squarely on the shoulders of the referred pupil who ended up doing an awful lot of the work in isolation and out of the context of where the problems appeared to manifest themselves.

(Tim Joyce)

Our experience of working with the many 'Freds' with whom we have come into contact over the years, suggests that as long as so much of the onus is on a pupil to adjust his or her behaviour to fit in with the school's scheme of things, the chances of successful long-term assimilation are small. If there is to be any hope of interrupting the self-reproducing process of rejection and response or preventing it from getting underway in the first place, then schools, as well as pupils, must be prepared to adapt and change. Schools must accept their own responsibility for examining *how* the dynamics of schooling may be contributing to 'problem behaviour', and *what* might be done both to ease the problems pupils are currently experiencing and, where possible, to prevent the same problems arising with the next generation of pupils.

Identifying features of schools' organisation and curricula, which might be adapted or improved to promote more constructive patterns of behaviour, is undoubtedly that much easier at one or more removes from the sometimes threatening immediacy of the classroom. Teachers like ourselves, who have chosen to work with 'problem' pupils, find that we are uniquely placed to look back in at the curriculum *from their point of view.*

(Mongon *et al.*, 1989, pp. 34–6)

2.79 Some classroom teachers would argue that as soon as the pressures of classroom teaching are relinquished it becomes impossible to understand education from *their* point of view.

2.80 In this section I asked 'when and why is education difficult?' I started by looking at when and why learning is difficult and attempted to draw on your experiences of difficulties in learning in order to define them for yourself. I argued that it made little sense to think of difficulties in learning as the province of a small group of students who are relatively low in attainment. I used the example of a science lesson to indicate the way any group of students can have difficulties in learning, if they are not helped to understand what they are expected to learn. I then considered the way official documents have pushed us to think of the difficulties of students as confined to a group *having* 'special needs' or 'learning difficulties'. I called into question the sense of estimating the numbers in such categories and took you through the definitions in the 1993 Education Act.

2.81 I then explored the difficulties students face from another angle by looking at a number of groups who may find education difficult; children in care, young people affected by HIV and AIDS, and traveller children. I suggested that all such students, as well as others, might face discrimination or devaluation outside and inside schools and pointed out the way devaluation could interfere with learning.

2.82 The section ended with an examination of the teacher and student perspectives on a single conflict in a secondary school.

3 HOW DO SCHOOLS RESPOND TO DIVERSITY?

3.1 How should schools be organized so that difficulties in learning are minimized? How should they respond to the diversity of their students? How should curricula be presented? In this section I will concentrate on attempts to answer these questions in two schools; the Grove Primary School in Cambridge and Whitmore High School in Harrow. Both these schools include young people with disabilities who come from quite a wide area. I will provide a contrasting example of a child with Down's syndrome attending a local rural primary school. Many of the issues I raise will be looked at in greater detail in Units 6/7 and 8/9.

3.2 Bernard Fairhurst taught environmental science in Gloucestershire. Like teachers in the Grove and Whitmore schools, he argues that shared experiences in mixed attainment groups can form the basis for differentiated teaching and learning. As part of his plan to involve his school and its community in environmental science he developed a mixed-habitat area:

38

I was able to get support and guidance from the horticultural adviser, a grant from the Nature Conservancy Council and design work and labouring by the pupils. Initial stages involved showing students the bit of school field, identifying the range of plants present and discussing how variety could be increased. Then drawing scale plans with the pupils designing a mixed-habitat area with all possible inclusions coming from them, e.g. pond, marsh, grassland, shrubs. As well as looking at the area, I prompted them with questions, e.g., 'How would you encourage amphibians? … reptiles? … flying mammals? … hedgehogs? … butterflies?' These provoked further thoughts and additions to plans. The questions, 'What about access for people in wheelchairs? Or plants for people who are visually impaired?' provoked various responses from interest and appreciating the need to rethink access, pathways, height of beds, varieties etc., to, 'What has that got to do with a habitat area?' or 'What has that got to do with our school?' We discussed the role of the school in providing a service to all the community. Students begin to see that in a small area a large range of plants and animals can be encouraged through careful management and gain an insight into ecological relationships. Feeders and bird and bat boxes could be built, flowers and shrubs planted for scent and nectar …

(Personal communication)

3.3   Environmental science, besides providing an infinite variety of fruitful shared experiences for students, is also a fertile source of metaphors for education and society. For some, the study of the natural world may bring to mind a competitive struggle for survival, and this may be seen as a suitable model for schools and classrooms. Others may see the role of teachers as more akin to an expert gardener creating an environment, with careful planning and regular intervention, in which a diversity of plants and animals can flourish.

UNDER THE WALNUT TREE: THE GROVE PRIMARY SCHOOL

3.4   The first television programme for this course is called *Under the Walnut Tree* (the tree is to be found in the central courtyard of the school) and is a documentary about the evolution of Grove Primary School in Cambridge. To support and extend the film, I have written a detailed account of the school which is Chapter 1 in Reader 2. I hope you will read this account *after* you have watched the programme to maximize its dramatic impact. The written account about the Grove should help you consider and react to the issues that are raised, but the chapter does not replace the film and you are strongly urged to watch the programme. This course is partly about examining and criticizing educational television; about exploring the impact of the images and arguments it contains.

3.5   In Thomas Hardy's novel, *Under the Greenwood Tree*, the tree bears witness to the passing generations in a manner reminiscent of the opening of a book for children. It has relevance, therefore, for a story about a primary school:

> Many hundreds of birds had been born amidst the boughs of this single tree; tribes of rabbits and hares had nibbled at its bark from year to year; quaint tufts of fungi had sprung from the cavities of its forks; and countless families of earthworms had crept about its roots. Beneath and beyond its shade spread a carefully-tended grass-plot, its purpose being to supply a healthy exercise-ground for young chickens and pheasants.

> (Hardy, 1872; p. 205 of the paperback edition)

3.6   I thought I was making a reference only to Hardy in my title for the television programme and chapter but I should have realized that the archaeological imperative, that turning over a stone always reveals something underneath, applies here too. As the introduction to my edition of *Under the Greenwood Tree* tells me, Hardy was making a reference to a sixteenth- or seventeenth-century ballad, 'describing rustic merrymaking':

O how they firk it, caper and jerk it
Under the greenwood tree.

3.7   I leave you to decide for yourselves on the appropriateness to education of the resonances of this refrain.

Activity 11   Pictures from the Grove

I hope that you can arrange your study of this unit so that you can watch TV1, *Under the Walnut Tree*, at this point. It would be useful to watch it with other course members so that you can pool your reactions. If you have the opportunity to record the programme so that you can stop and start it on a second run through, so much the better. *Write down and, if possible, discuss your reactions to the programme.* What did it remind you about? Do not feel constrained, here, to stick to the themes of the programme but be aware when you are not. Watching a programme like this can prompt reflections in many directions. It may link into an element of your experience or ideas you would wish to explore further. Jot down these tangential links then concentrate more specifically on the programme's content. What did you learn from it? What would you like to know more about?

3.8   Did you resist learning from and about the subject matter of the programme? A council-built estate in Cambridge is not inner-city London or Glasgow or Belfast or Cardiff. It is not rural Yorkshire or Cornwall. It is one particular place and could not be anything else. We were not trying to pick an 'easy setting' to demonstrate the virtues of inclusive educational policies, nor to say that the way education has developed in this setting is the best it could have been. However, we have tried to explain why the school has developed in the way it has.

3.9   The making of the programme has its own story. I selected the Grove school to introduce many of the issues of the course. I also chose it because it is near my home and I want to encourage you to get to know and begin to study your own areas. It seems sensible to make this a shared task. My first ideas were for a more ambitious programme about the various communities connected to the Grove; of pupils, school workers, parents and the surrounding estate. I wanted, too, to examine the pressure on schools to become suppliers of attractive commodities, in competition with others for the patronage of their customers, rather than an integral part of the life of the surrounding community. I realized, however, that this would require a series to itself, rather than a single 25-minute programme. The scaled-down project is still large enough to mean that little is examined in depth.

3.10   There is not a great deal of detail about the disabilities of the pupils in the programme. We saw the pupils as part of the audience for the programme and wished to avoid talking about any of the pupils as if they were objects of study. Even so, you may feel that the pupils with disabilities receive too much attention in the film. When you take a camera crew into a school where there are children with disabilities there is a tendency for the crew to assume that the film will be about disability; for the camera to linger on a child with disabilities rather than the learning of another class member. We tried to minimize this during the shooting and editing of the film. Did we succeed?

3.11   I suspect that your viewing of the programme will leave many loose ends. What does a particular worker do? What difficulties does a particular pupil experience? What did the pupils learn on the trip?

Activity 12   The book of the film

Now read 'Under the walnut tree: the Grove Primary School', Chapter 1 in Reader 2. As you go through it, write down the questions it raises for you. What does it add to the programme? What is still omitted? Near the beginning I set out three aims: to portray a school, pupils and staff that have a past and a future; to sample the curriculum; and to examine the way pupils with disabilities are included within the school. Are these aims adequate? Are they fulfilled?

3.12   The chapter is quite long, yet it only scratches the surface of the life of the school. However, most issues raised in the chapter will have been given more thorough attention by the end of the course.

Activity 13   What would you choose to study next?

Make a list of those aspects of education raised by my account of the Grove that you might wish to find out more about. What, if anything, captured your interest?

3.13   My list, which reflects my particular interests, may bear little resemblance to yours. it would include:

- the history of open-air schools (see below);
- the position and training of learning support assistants (these are called welfare assistants in TV1 and the reader chapter but see their new job title as more accurately reflecting their activities);
- the national trends in the education of pupils with physical disabilities and visual disabilities;
- the use of microtechnology with pupils with disabilities;
- the integration of pupils at secondary schools;
- techniques of physiotherapy, including conductive education;
- inconsistency in LEA policies;
- speech therapy, which is not discussed in my account;

- curriculum approaches across the school;
- approaches to gender and class;
- attitudes to ability;
- the multicultural content of the curriculum.

Activity 14 An open-air school

Appendix 2 is a description of the Roger Ascham School taken from *The Cambridge Chronicle and University Journal* for 1930. I obtained it from the local history collection at the central library in Cambridge. It describes the school a few years after it first opened and is included here to indicate a start that could be made to a local historical study. As you read it, consider how you might begin a historical project in your local area. What would you like to find out about? Whom might you interview?

Roger Ascham, a special school for children with physical disabilities, now closed. Originally its pavilions were built to provide an open-air education for pupils said to be 'delicate' in health or 'backward' in ability.

Curriculum and classroom support

3.14   My portrait of the curriculum of the Grove is very selective. There are thirteen class teachers in the school and I included three of them. In TV1, besides the rat, rocks and fen-life, there are two further lessons, a pottery lesson and a music and singing lesson. We did not suggest to teachers what should be shown on screen but we discussed what lessons were being considered and selected from them. Each lesson indicates how a shared starting point can be used as the basis for further work, closely related to the particular interests and competence of each student.

Activity 15   Building on past experience

How would you develop the lesson based on Tim Lister's fossil collection? Look at the subjects of the national curriculum for England and Wales (below) and jot down six tasks or activities in which groups of students might engage, which draw on one or any combination of these subjects. If you are in Scotland you may wish to think in terms of the curriculum areas of the 5–14 programme: English language, mathematics, environmental studies, expressive arts, personal and social development, and religious and moral education (Brown, 1994). If you are in Northern Ireland you may prefer to consider the areas of study of the 4–16 curriculum: English, mathematics, science and technology, environment and society, creative and expressive studies, and language studies (for secondary schools).

The structure of the National Curriculum [for England and Wales]

The National Curriculum applies to pupils of compulsory school age in maintained schools, including grant-maintained and grant-maintained special schools. It is organised on the basis of four *key stages*, which are broadly as follows:

	Pupils' ages	*Year groups*
Key stage 1	5–7	1–2
Key stage 2	7–11	3–6
Key stage 3	11–14	7–9
Key stage 4	14–16	10–11

In England, the following *subjects* are included in the National Curriculum at the key stages shown:

Key stages 1 and 2	English, mathematics, science, technology (design and technology, and information technology), history, geography, art, music, and physical education
Key stage 3	as at key stages 1 and 2, plus a modern foreign language
Key stage 4	English, mathematics, and science; from August 1995, physical education; and, from August 1996, technology (design and technology, and information technology) and a modern foreign language.

For each subject and for each key stage, *programmes of study* set out what pupils should be taught and *attainment targets* set out the expected standards of pupils' performance.

(DFE, 1995, p. v)

Responsibility for the curriculum

3.15   In the Grove the class teacher has overall responsibility for the curriculum. Sometimes, though not always, the support teachers have no warning of the content of a lesson. In other schools such as Whitmore, described below, there may be a greater emphasis on joint planning.

Supporting pupils' learning

3.16   The pupils at the Grove are all members of mainstream classes; though, as the account makes clear, when the pupils with visual disabilities were first part of the school, they spent most of their time in their own unit. In other schools pupils may still be educated in this way. At Impington Village College, where pupils with physical disabilities transfer at eleven, several of the pupils spend part of their time in the purpose-built 'pavilion'.

3.17   At some schools, too, the provision for supporting pupils with disabilities is thought of as separate from the support for other pupils who may experience difficulties in learning. This is not so at the Grove. All pupils who experience difficulties are helped within the same support network. The changes that have taken place in such practices more generally mirror the developments at the Grove. Withdrawal teaching has decreased and has been replaced by support in the classroom, though this has not been universally applied nor embraced wholeheartedly by all the staff in the schools in which it has occurred. Under either system the support available is often inadequate. The practice of learning support will be explored further in the discussion of Whitmore High School and in Unit 6/7.

3.18   The number of learning support assistants in the school is above the national norm for the support of pupils with disabilities in the mainstream, but it is not above the numbers available in the nearby special schools. Thelma's lesson contained four adults all busily supporting the pupils. If such numbers were available could they be profitably occupied in all lessons?

3.19   Sometimes the constant close attention of a learning support assistant may be seen as creating dependence and of getting in the way of pupils' independence, co-operative learning and social relationships. Could pupils negotiate the level of support they should receive? How should one balance the needs for support with the needs for independence and privacy? How might this change with the age of students?

Scenes from the Grove: friendship, food, concentration, visits, community ...

Scenes from the Grove: support, playing together, discussing work.

3.20   The job of a learning support assistant is a complex one but is not highly paid. After I completed the chapter for the reader, it transpired that the learning support assistants at the Grove were not after all going to be given parity with their colleagues in special schools. The LEA had entered into an agreement with the union that the special school learning support assistants were to be paid more. This must make arguments about the transfer of pupils and resources from special schools into the mainstream more fraught, as well as undermining an already vulnerable group of staff. In 1991 the county council started looking at the savings that could be made by reducing the support provided to pupils with disabilities in the mainstream. Grove school was told that they would have only seven instead of fourteen learning support assistants. Eventually the teachers and governors won the argument to retain their previous staffing levels. But any new cut in the county budget may threaten staffing levels.

Policies towards children with disabilities

3.21   What did you feel about the nature of the policy process portrayed in TV1 and Chapter 1 of Reader 2? There was some degree of planning but much depended on circumstance and fortune. The shaping of educational policy by fire is unlikely to be adopted generally. However, when a special school comes to the end of its life the policy alternatives are brought sharply into focus. Should the school be rebuilt or should the money be spent to support the same students in the mainstream?

3.22   You may question the concentration of pupils with disabilities in a single, 'special' mainstream school. Could more be done to support pupils with disabilities to attend their local schools? Does the school act like a magnet, drawing resources and expertise away from these communities? Earlier in the unit I gave a definition of integration as 'the process of increasing the participation of students in the educational and social life of mainstream schools'. Should we add a word here and talk of integration as 'the process of increasing the participation of students in neighbourhood mainstream schools'?

Activity 16   Centralizing resources

What are the advantages and disadvantages of centralizing resources at the Grove? How could the resources be distributed differently between the Grove and schools more local to the disabled students?

3.23   Arguments for centralizing resources may refer, among other things, to avoiding travelling of specialist staff, sharing expertise of specialist staff, sharing equipment and the adaptations of buildings and the solidarity of students facing similar difficulties. Arguments against centralization might include the maintenance of relationships in the local community, minimizing travel for students, reducing the likelihood of seeing students as a group rather than as individuals, providing more students with the opportunity to have a disabled classmate, making more schools face up to the access difficulties of school buildings and curriculum. You might well add arguments to either of these lists.

3.24   Some LEAs have made a more co-ordinated effort to effect changes in their schools than others. (See Reader 2, Chapter 32, 'Integration policy in Newham, 1986–90' by Linda Jordan.) Most have built up their provision in piecemeal fashion depending on the particular interests of education officers and local authority councillors, as well as the pressures from individual schools, parents and central government. Why do you think LEAs have found large-scale planning so difficult? The 1988 and 1993 Education Acts have severely curtailed LEA powers to develop coherent policies, but in many areas policies were not well articulated before these interventions.

3.25   The planning of support for students within an LEA is affected by its geography. From the point of view of the planners in a mixture of rural and urban communities it may seem sensible to centralize resources in towns. However, to parents or pupils in villages, daily travel to and from the nearest town may be unacceptable.

Activity 17   An achievement to be proud of

In Reader 1, Chapter 12, Alyson Clare, the headteacher, has described the progress made by Chris Raine at her village school in Ravenstonedale in the Lake District. Chris has Down's syndrome or trisomy 21 (which means that he was born with an extra 21st chromosome). Before you start the reading jot down your response to the following questions:

• What ideas do you have about the capabilities of children with Down's syndrome?

• What would be the advantages and disadvantages of including a child with Down's syndrome in his or her local primary school:

– from the child's point of view?

– from the parents' point of view?

– from the point of view of other children at the school?

– from the point of view of teachers and other schoolworkers?

– from the point of view of local authority administrators?

Now read the chapter and consider:

• the nature and appropriateness of the support offered to Chris;

• the advantages and disadvantages of attendance at a local school as opposed to a centralized resource in a mainstream school;

• whether and how your preconceptions are modified by your reading.

3.26   Alyson Clare and Chris's teacher show a knack for turning the support they offer Chris into an educational opportunity for other children. Thus the whole school join in the learning of Makaton, a signing vocabulary based on British Sign Language, as well as the finger-spelling of letters of the alphabet. In helping Chris to develop the structure of his utterances they are likely to increase their own knowledge of syntax. The attention to and tolerance towards the educational requirements of one individual form a model which could be applied to any child. Is such a concentration on Chris likely to diminish or enhance an ability in schoolworkers and pupils for meeting the educational needs of others?

3.27   I know little about *your* expectations and how they may have been modified by reading the account. However, I have met people, including professionals, who find it difficult to accept that children with Down's syndrome may have developed powers of concentration and have an interest in books and reading. People with the syndrome are very varied in their interests and abilities. Some have profound and multiple disabilities. Others are capable, like Chris, of making considerable and rapid educational progress.

3.28   In the late 1970s I was involved with a group of parents who wanted to obtain a mainstream education for their five-year-old children with Down's syndrome. Whenever I visit Cambridge University Library I am reminded of the low expectations some in the local authority held out for 'William' (Booth and Statham, 1982). He is now in his twenties and works in the library tea-room.

3.29   More recently Alice Paige-Smith and I have been involved in documenting the inclusion of students with Down's syndrome in mainstream secondary schools in eight local education authorities. The inclusion rates in secondary schools range from 2 per cent to 50 per cent in these authorities. Such differences must depend on local policies rather than the characteristics of students. We are calling the report of this research, ironically, 'Rhyme or reason?', since from the point of view of parents and students there is no sensible justification for the struggles they have to obtain a mainstream place in some areas.

Young people with Down's syndrome in mainstream secondary schools

Peter in Buckinghamshire

Claire in Derbyshire

Robert in Cambridgeshire

Annette in Oxfordshire

Peter's support assistant sits alongside him. Mark, in wheelchair, is seated next to them. How might the arrangements be changed to maximize participation?

Activity 18 How far can you go?

There are two special schools in the vicinity of the Grove. One caters for pupils said to have 'severe learning difficulties', the other for pupils categorized as having 'moderate learning difficulties'. Children given these labels are very varied in their performance but some students categorized as having 'severe learning difficulties' may not use oral or sign language or computer-assisted language in communication. Their communications may be limited to the most rudimentary body language.

What characteristics prevent students from supported participation within a mainstream school?

3.30 My view is that there are very few students currently in special schools who could not attend mainstream schools with support. The particular pupils that are excluded depends on chance factors and the preconceptions and misconceptions of those with the power to initiate policy changes. I have two sorts of reasons for thinking this. One set refers to my experience. I have seen pupils incorporated effectively within mainstream primary and secondary schools irrespective of the severity of their disability or the difficulties they have with learning. The other set is conceptual. The most common arguments in favour of special schools are really arguments for centralization of resources and, as the Grove illustrates, resources can be centralized within a mainstream school.

3.31   There are two legitimate arguments for segregation. The separating
or isolation of students in their own school can be seen as bringing
positive educational benefits, over and above the centralization of
resources. Alternatively they may be thought to require segregation in
order to protect the education of others. The first argument is put
forward forcefully by some teachers of the deaf and by some deaf adults
who feel that the relative isolation of students is the only way to create a
thriving signing community. In Unit 6/7 you will encounter attempts to
support signing in the mainstream and will then be in a better position to
judge this argument. The second argument is put forward in relation to
the small number of students who are excluded from mainstream schools
for persistent violent behaviour. The numbers involved, the means to
keep these to a minimum, and the appropriate subsequent action will be
addressed in Unit 11/12.

Activity 19   What is a special school?

In what I have written so far I have talked of special schools as schools
which are physically separate from the mainstream. Under Part III of the
1993 Education Act special schools are defined as schools which are
'specially organized to make special education provision for pupils with
special educational needs' (Education Act 1993, clause 182). Under this
definition, would the Grove be a special school? What about
Ravenstonedale school attended by Chris Raine? What about any
mainstream school well organized to support students who experience
difficulties in learning?

3.32   You or I might wish to call the Grove or Ravenstonedale special
schools. Such a view is reflected in the title of Tony Dessent's book,
Making the Ordinary School Special (Dessent, 1987). However, the 1993 Act
specifically excludes such mainstream schools from the definition of
special schools by saying that a special school is a school 'not being a
maintained or grant-maintained school' (Education Act 1993, clause 188).
The fact that special schools can be either maintained or grant-maintained
special schools makes this definition particularly confusing. So officially
the only schools that can be special schools are ones which *only* take
students who have been categorized as having 'special needs'. The
situation is further complicated by the practice in some local authorities
(Oxfordshire and Leicestershire for example) to set up primary
departments of special schools within a mainstream primary school and
secondary departments within a mainstream secondary school. The
education of a student might be supported within mainstream classes as
at the Grove, but officially the child will be said to attend a 'special'
school. In this course we will use the term 'special school' with its official
meaning, but you should be aware of how the existence of 'special
mainstream schools' undermines the argument for retaining official
'special schools'.

Compulsory segregation

3.33   Official 'special schools' are not defined, then, by the support they provide but by their exclusivity. They are selective schools. They also have another significant attribute. Although parents, at least in theory, now have a considerable say in where a child officially categorized as 'having special needs' is educated, the choice of a mainstream school can be overridden. Once a special school is indicated on a Statement as the place of education, then attendance is compulsory. Compulsory segregation can be seen to be the real defining feature of special schools. For if they took students who *opted* to attend them they would attract students on the same basis as other schools. In the terminology of some local authorities they would be specialized or 'magnet' mainstream schools, drawing students to them on the basis of the kind of education they offer.

Compulsory integration

3.34   The choice of parents to have their child educated in a 'special' school may be overridden too. Where a policy choice has been made to transfer the resources from a special school into mainstream schools one could argue that in that area compulsory integration is in operation. Just as in an area where there are no grammar schools or City Technology Colleges one might suggest that comprehensive schooling is compulsory, although there might well be the option of private education. Any educational system provides a range of options, excludes others, and limits choice within it, for example, according to age. In considering policies about education you should consider what options should be provided and what power should be given to parents and students in deciding between them.

Secondary transfer: Impington Village College

3.35   Impington Village College, to which children with physical disabilities transfer from the Grove, was the culmination of Henry Morris's project for a network of village colleges. He was Chief Education Officer of Cambridgeshire from 1922 to 1954 and set out his vision for rural education in a memorandum published by Cambridge University Press in 1925. He provides a reminder of the role schools can play in the lives of communities:

> The village college would change the whole face of the problem of rural education. As the community centre of the neighbourhood it would provide for the whole man [sic], and abolish the duality of education and ordinary life. It would not only be the training ground for the art of living, but the place in which life is lived, the environment of a genuine corporate life. The dismal dispute of vocational and non-vocational education would not arise in it. It would be a visible demonstration in stone of the continuity and never ceasingness of education. There would be no 'leaving school'! – the child would enter at three and leave the college only in extreme old age. (In all seriousness it might be said that the 'school leaving age' would be lifted to 90.) It would have the great virtue of being local so that it would enhance the quality of actual life as it is lived from day to day – the supreme object of education.
>
> (Morris, 1925, p. 154)

3.36   Such a vision of education runs counter to the emphasis, in Conservative legislation, on schools competing for students from the communities of other schools. And for the disabled students, Impington is unlikely to be their local school.

3.37   Some Impington staff feared that students with disabilities would be unable to cope with the standard of work expected in secondary school and wanted to exclude some on the basis of their low attainment. There were fears that Madeleine Norman (featured in TV1) might find it difficult to cope with the school despite her relatively high levels of achievement. There is a reluctance on the part of some secondary teachers to accept the accuracy of primary school reports about pupils. Sometimes this can work in the pupil's favour when they discard an unwarranted reputation or are given a fresh start. At other times it can condemn them to work again through material they have already covered. In Madeleine's case, despite the careful efforts at liaison by the Grove, there seemed to be a limited understanding of her skills with information technology for a while after she started Impington. She was made to use a concept keyboard which involved less sophisticated technology and language than she had used with her light-talker. Nevertheless, when Jonathan Croall visited Impington Village College for the *Times Educational Supplement* in May 1991, Madeleine featured as one of the successes of the school's integration policy.

Activities at Impington: pupils with disabilities are involved in a wide range of activities in mainstream classes. Shown here are English, textiles and science, as well as a view into a classroom in the 'Pavilion'.

Madeleine in her science lesson.

I watched a group of two dozen year 7 students doing a science experiment which involved pouring silver nitrate into salty and distilled water. Among them was Madeleine Norman who ... has cerebral palsy and is in a wheelchair. Two able-bodied students were working alongside her. Her teacher, Toni Woodcock, adds: 'Madeleine's very active and knows what's going on. The other kids are brilliant, they really share with her. But it's a delicate balance – between getting her involved, and allowing her to see things happening.'

Striking the right balance is also important in relation to attitudes. On a wall in the Pavilion, as part of a student project on cerebral palsy, I found the statement: 'If people want to understand me, the first thing they've got to do is forget about my disability and talk to me as a person. Then they'll realise I'm just like anyone else.' ...

One testing-ground for equality of treatment is discipline. Staff say they try to be even-handed in dealing with anti-social behaviour. 'The disabled students can be just as naughty and irritating as the others,' Sylvia West says, remembering an occasion when she had to cram several wheelchairs and occupants into her office for a reprimand. In most schools you hear the traditional 'No running!' call from teachers. At Impington you hear 'No wheelies!'

But do the students themselves feel they are treated equally? Lisa Garrett, a cheerful 15-year-old with a 'Kick Ass!' sticker on the arm of her wheelchair has no doubts: 'I don't feel any different from the others. Most students accept you: they're helpful, but they don't show they're treating you differently.'

Oliver Dann has rather more mixed feelings. A bright, fairly outspoken 13-year-old, he thinks the school is 'pretty good'. He likes mixing with able-bodied students – several are his friends – and going to normal lessons. 'But some of the first-years treat me as if I was an idiot or a bit thick, as if I wasn't normal. I'd like to change that attitude.'

The able-bodied students I spoke to seemed quite clear and unsentimental about the issue. Amongst a group of 14-year-olds, one boy said: 'You don't feel embarrassed now when you see disabled people in the streets.' Another boy agreed: 'It's not strange, it's normal – but we still think of them as disabled.' A third said he didn't often talk to the disabled students. When I asked why, he said he didn't know – 'you're asking me things that make me realise I haven't thought very deeply about it.' …

(Jonathan Croall, *Times Educational Supplement*, 31 May 1991)

WHITMORE HIGH SCHOOL

3.38   The changes that have taken place at Whitmore High School, in Harrow, parallel the developments at the Grove in many respects. The teachers have devised a unified system to support the learning of all pupils. They have broadened their community to include students with disabilities. Perhaps they have gone further than the Grove school in making explicit the nature of the changes they want to see and the philosophy underlying them as well as in encouraging the whole school to adopt them. Primary teachers might argue that as secondary teachers they actually had further to go before they could claim to be making the curriculum responsive to individual students.

Activity 20   Wholesale changes

Chapter 2 of Reader 2 is called 'A curricular response to diversity at Whitmore High School'. It is written by Christine Gilbert, who was then the headteacher, and by Michael Hart, the head of learning support, now known as learning development. Read the chapter up to the end of section 2 (pp. 38–44). These first two sections describe the way the whole school was involved in change, and the nature of the approach to learning support which they introduced.

As you read the first two sections of the chapter consider the following:

*   What might prevent the involvement of a whole school in policy development?

*   What might be the objections to organizing learning support in the ways suggested?

- The support for children's learning at Whitmore is based at the school. In other places some support is provided on demand by an authority-wide learning support service. What are the advantages and disadvantages of school-based and 'peripatetic' services?

A whole-school response

3.39   For some of you, the idea of all the staff of a school pulling in the same direction may seem entirely alien. You may be more used to schools in which there are as many points of view as there are members of staff. At the Grove, Thelma Jopling divided the staff into the progressives, the traditionalists and those in between 'who sit in meetings and say little'. We are not given details of the struggles and arguments at Whitmore, though in a 1,000 pupil secondary school with a large staff there must have been some. Who wins such struggles depends on who has the power and who can muster the most support. As head Christine Gilbert was in a strong position to initiate changes and was able to gain support for them by representing them as part of the effort to stave off a threat of closure.

3.40   The changes were supported by the local authority through its 1986 'learning support policy' and the local authority special needs advisers (Gilbert and Hart, 1990). The policy was opposed by a headteacher of one of the local special schools who 'mounted an energetic campaign against the policy document'. The LEA started to transfer money into the mainstream that had been used previously to pay for students with disabilities to attend residential special schools. The progress of this integration policy can be seen in Table 1. The figures show a large net movement from residential to mainstream provision with a slight drop in numbers at Harrow's special schools.

Table 1   School attendance of students with statements in Harrow (aged 2–19)

	March 1986	January 1987	September 1989
Borough special school	254	237	210
Borough mainstream school	83	92	216
Out borough special school (day)	109	104	77
Out borough special school (residential)	118	106	49

(Source: adapted from Gilbert and Hart, 1990, p. 108)

3.41   Some of you may work in schools where the approach to overcoming difficulties in learning differs from that at Whitmore. It might seem that a new orthodoxy is being proposed which ignores the benefits of your method of working. Some teachers are very wary of giving up what they see as the advantages of direct teaching of pupils who experience difficulties, away from the scene of their failure.

3.42   Hellen Matthews, then a principal teacher in a secondary school in Aberdeen, wrote a brief account of her reactions to policy changes in her region of Scotland (Matthews, 1987). She records how, following a period when withdrawal from lessons was to be avoided at all costs, she came to regard it as having a value for particular purposes, observing that 'after all, pupils are still withdrawn repeatedly for individual music lessons'.

> Now, when we discuss 'withdrawal' within this region we are speaking about precisely which settings are most appropriate for support in class, either in a quiet area of the classroom or in another room. The decisions made should be common-sense ones, taking account of the following kinds of consideration:
>
> 1   How easily distracted is the pupil with the tasks in hand?
>
> 2   Will the dialogue which the pupil and I shall share interfere with other talk going on in the classroom? Will our work be distracting to the other teacher or the rest of the class, either because of conversations cutting across each other or because the rest of the class is working quietly?
>
> 3   Will being overheard possibly embarrass the pupil being helped?
>
> The fact that the pupil may for some reason (e.g. prolonged absence) be doing completely different work is not in itself a sufficient reason for removing to another room, and pressure to do this becomes less where teaching-styles permit group or individual learning.
> (Matthews, 1987, p. 194–5)

3.43   She decided that science laboratory work never merited withdrawal, but she did withdraw students for French revision or where groups of students encountered similar difficulties in mathematics.

3.44   The changes in approach to learning support in Aberdeen were supported by clear guidelines from the local authority and from Scottish HMI. National guidelines for training courses were established so that a switch in approach would be reinforced (see Unit 6/7 and Fordyce, 1987). However, as an evaluation study has reported, the advocated practices have been taken up to varying extents in schools:

> Co-operative teaching between learning support staff and subject or classroom teachers was found to be common; extraction of pupils

from mainstream classes was relatively rare in secondary schools, but practised widely in the primary sector.

(Allan, Brown and Munn, 1991, p. 92)

3.45   In many local authorities the provision of learning support is not based in particular schools but in a peripatetic 'support service for special educational needs'. How can support teachers be an integral part of developments within a school if they are based outside it? Her Majesty's Inspectorate published a report of a survey of such support services in 1989. They found that often these services did not work closely with schools to produce a coherent policy on difficulties in learning:

> The majority of new services are based on peripatetic teams already working for the LEA. These teams generally consisted of remedial teachers who had worked with schools towards particular goals, e.g. assisting pupils with reading problems … Too often classroom teachers reported confusing or conflicting advice from different advisory groups, for example about oral work, the grouping of pupils and the adaptation of teaching methods … the general picture was one of fragmentation, with advisory services lacking common objectives.
>
> (DES, 1989, pp. 4–6)

3.46   Fred Sedgwick has written more bluntly about the difficulty of fitting in a visitor, who expects to tackle the learning difficulty of a pupil, into the unpredictable life of a school:

> **On the outside looking in …**
>
> Sam, who is six, came to me in agony. He's had various kinds of pain in his life so far …
>
> Sam's agony today was a creamy spotty lump outside a lower tooth. Biting on his playtime apple had started it off, and for ten minutes his wailing was unrelenting. Then Sue, the secretary, calmed him down with building bricks and other interesting plastic things cadged from the nursery for just this sort of purpose. And no doubt the hurt went away as the pressure subsided.
>
> I rang school health for advice. Our nurse and her superior (I use the fashionable line management term) were on courses, so I tried the local dental clinic, and wonderfully, Sam was one of their patients; even better, they would see him straightaway.
>
> But while this was going on, the visiting special needs teacher had turned up. Distracted by the noise from his systematic search for specific learning difficulties attached, however tenuously, to immature humans, he had found Sam. Taken him on his knee. Comforted him. And this had brought the yelling on, with a new vigour.
>
> As Sue forced Sam's coat on, the special needs teacher asked me which children I would like him to see. He meant, were there any

possible dyslexics about the place, and I resisted saying 'Here's a special need – sort this one out'. I was putting on my jacket at this point. Sam, quietened again by Sue, was waiting placidly ...

Eventually Sam and I got out to my car. At the dentist's it appeared he'd missed his last appointment. An abscess was diagnosed, and he was given antibiotics. I had lunch with him back at school, to make sure he had something soft – mince – and we both showed off our stickers: 'Hip hip hooray, no more decay'. I usually promise myself a salad and end up with chips. That's what happened today. Nursery crisis, nursery food.

When I got back to the office, the special needs teacher was at my side again. 'What children do you want me to see?' He always treats me as if he were the only person in the school I have to deal with. And our poor relationship, which is at least half my fault, is more than a personal clash: it underlines the deep gap that exists in thinking about special needs provision. On the one side are the basic-skillers, still talking almost entirely about phonics. On the other, those who want to broaden the action visiting teachers might take to include the whole curriculum, not to mention needs that can be defined only in human, not educational terms.

The first kind still takes children from their friends, the second keeps them together. The first concentrates on a part of the curriculum that the teacher and the child both know he or she can't cope with; the second sees the child as entitled to the whole curriculum, whatever his or her ability.

One of the first kind commented in our staffroom recently: 'Of course the children were more interested in what was going on around them than in my sentences'. Jeanette, my teacher, said, 'he should make his bloody sentences more interesting then, shouldn't he?'

The basic-skillers ply their trade in opposition to what bits of human life might be going on. I wish they'd see the business of being human in some coherent way, instead of fragmented into tables and test results. As our one fussed about while we were looking after Sam, he reminded me of a man who called at a house: 'Can I see Mr. Brown?' 'I'm afraid,' says the solemn man inside the front door, 'Mr. Brown died this morning. I am his brother and this [a weeping women in the hallway] is his widow.' 'Oh,' says the caller. 'Did he say anything about a pot of paint?'

(Sedgewick, 1988, p. 21)

3.47   We will return to the value and future of support services in Unit 14/15. In the financial circumstances of the early 1990s they appear to be under threat. Throughout the 1980s many teachers witnessed the cutting back of support staff (Gipps, Gross and Goldstein, 1987). For some of you the practices of learning support may seem a luxury of the past.

From learning support to learning development

3.48 The title change from 'learning support' teachers to 'learning development' teachers emphasized a significant change in role. Such teachers were to share in planning and teaching. In seeking for ways in which solutions to the difficulties of some students might benefit all students, this gave them an important role in curriculum development in the school.

Activity 21 From learning support to curriculum development ———

The development of learning support at Whitmore is summarized well in Table 2.2 on page 43 of Gilbert and Hart's chapter (Reader 2 Chapter 2). The roles of support staff are described as varying along a continuum: from attention to the work of a single student, to joint planning, teaching and assessment with the subject teacher for all students in a class. The rest of the chapter looks at the benefits of such totally shared responsibility, or team-teaching, for the effectiveness of teaching and the development of curricula. It shows how the examination of possible improvements led to new ways of working in a number of subject departments.

The teachers in this school were committed to using team work to improve the teaching of groups with a wide mix of attainment. Read the rest of the chapter and consider whether such an approach could be taken equally to support the development of teaching of students grouped according to high, low and intermediate levels of attainment.

3.49 The extent to which students should be grouped according to attainment has always been hotly debated. The proponents of either side of the debate like to argue that one approach leads to more effective teaching than the other. We will return to the issue in Unit 6/7 and Unit 11/12 as well as Unit 16. Some of the key questions in the debate are:

1   Who gains and who loses when class groups are divided according to attainment either between or within classes?

2   Does the division of students according to attainment mean that some students are more highly valued than others?

3   If some students are valued more highly than others and hence some students are 'devalued' does this interfere with their education or lead to disaffection?

4   Do different attainment tracks imply different curricular opportunities?

5   Can adequate opportunities be provided for moving between groups?

3.50 The debate about dividing classes according to attainment is clearly connected to arguments about withdrawal or in-classroom support. If you believe that classrooms should be divided according to attainment, does this recreate the need for a 'remedial class'?

3.51   You probably know which side of the debate I favour, though I do not decide it mainly on the basis of predicted educational outcomes. I think that systems which emphasize selection into homogeneous groups, or which stress the possibility of supporting the diversity of heterogeneous groups, can provide comparable educational results but that you choose between them based on the social organization you prefer. I see any highly selective educational or social and economic system as having costs in terms of the disaffection of those less highly valued and a heartless competitiveness on the part of those who succeed. Others see comprehensive systems, or systems emphasizing equality of value, as limiting opportunities for acquiring and manipulating power and wealth. I do not regard it as the task of a course like this to resolve issues of political belief. However, I think we have to ask ourselves whether our involvement with students who experience difficulties commits us to reducing those difficulties. Where they arise through social or educational devaluation, are we not committed to reducing such devaluation?

3.52   You can think of these disputes as connected to three related principles. A *comprehensive principle* is concerned with the education of pupils of diverse backgrounds and attainments together in primary and secondary schools. An *integration principle* is concerned with increasing the participation of children and young people who experience difficulties in learning or have disabilities within the mainstream of education. A *principle of equality of value* is concerned with the reduction of discrimination against children and young people in education on the basis of their background, gender, skin colour, ethnicity, attainments or disability. The first two of these have obvious counter-principles, of *selection* and *segregation*. I would argue that selection and segregation are bound up with the ascription of differences in value to students on the basis of their background, attainment and disability. You will have ample opportunity to examine and contest this assertion.

Developing mixed-attainment teaching

3.53   The development of methods for teaching diverse groups is at the heart of the changes at Whitmore. 'Mixed-attainment teaching' in secondary schools covers a number of practices. In this school it means the absence of setting by attainment as well as the absence of banding or streaming. Teaching through mixed-attainment groups for all years 7–11 is rare in secondary schools but the teachers at Whitmore feel they can provide group or individualized teaching for students in their first three years of school, as at the Grove. Thereafter, although 'each course in the school is open to all pupils', the nature of the courses involve some degree of guided self-selection.

3.54   However carefully selected, all groups contain students with a range of knowledge skills and experience and would benefit from the kind of attention given to teaching methods and curricula at Whitmore school. In the science lesson on radioactivity described in Section 2 each student experienced the lesson differently despite the fact that the teacher presented a single lesson to the whole class. A learning development co-teacher working with the science teacher might have helped both students and teacher towards a more productive use of their time.

SUMMARY

3.55   I have covered a multiplicity of issues in this section in varying degrees of detail. Through a case study of the Grove school I have looked at the way present practice in a school can be understood in terms of its history and the background of policy decisions within an LEA. I have examined the way curricula can be shared and differentiated. I have looked at learning support assistants and support teachers and alternatives to policies for centralizing support for children with disabilities. I have considered the difficulties that can arise at transfer to secondary school for children with disabilities. Through the case study of Whitmore High School I have introduced the notion of whole-school policies and changing approaches to learning support or learning 'development', from extraction to co-operative teaching to team teaching in mixed-attainment groups.

4 HOW SHOULD WE REACT TO GOVERNMENT POLICIES?

4.1   This section is based on a supplement in which we have placed the material most likely to date. You should read that now. Here I have provided you with some reminders of changes introduced by government and some reactions to them.

'Yes that's right – palpitations, irrationality, bed-wetting – and that's just the staff!'

School repairs working party minutes, continued: the headmaster, stressing his belief that money should be spent on books and not refurbishment, stamped his foot. Meeting closed.

5 HOW SHOULD WE SPEAK, WRITE AND READ?

5.1   In reading the course texts, watching the television programmes and listening to the audio-cassettes you may hear a number of strong voices. However, we do not want you to treat any of them as above suspicion. We hope you will examine carefully and criticize all aspects of the course as well as questioning your own ideas and the practices in education that you encounter. We hope that by the end of the course you will have become adept at teasing out and examining the hidden assumptions and in detecting and analysing contradictions in what is said and written about education.

5.2   For example, I have suggested that the course writers see the resolution of difficulties in learning as part of the task of creating an education system that is responsive to all learners. Is this a realistic aim? What are the limits of this approach? Are the interests of different groups of learners opposed, such that the reduction of difficulties for some involves the redirection of resources from others? If so, what principles should determine the way teaching and material resources are distributed within the systems of education? The course's title does not have a question mark. It is up to you to put one there and after any other assertion in the course.

5.3   One of my intentions in telling the story of an assembly at the start of this unit was to open a dialogue with you about the way all pupils might feel equally valued as members of a school community. Is it realistic to expect people to value equally the achievements of a student who gains three grade As at A-level and the halting communication of an eighteen-year-old categorized as having severe learning difficulties? Does an attempt to make all pupils feel valued involve the curbing of excellence? What would have to change within schools and society if a principle of equality of value were put into practice? What implications would such a principle have for wage and salary structures?

5.4   There are a number of barriers to understanding and evaluating what is going on in education and special education. We are all held back by our own limitations, by our previous convictions, by our comfort with unexamined ways of thinking that support our own needs and fantasies and our place within our culture and society.

5.5   But it is not only our own limitations which prevent us from coolly assessing the merits of arguments. It is a common, if disappointing, experience that when people acquire power they may come to believe that the acquisition of power in itself confers them with knowledge and sense. In fact the reverse process may occur. If you can win an argument by virtue of your position then you may be less scrupulous about the nature of the arguments you deploy. Some arguments carry authority over us even when we see their lack of sense. Thus there are reasons why challenging received wisdom may seem against our own interests. One of the students on the forerunner to this course concluded, after her critique of professional power relationships, that she had 'blown her chances of promotion for ever'.

5.6   In this brief section I will offer some structure for your critical reflections on the issues raised by this course and elsewhere. One of your assignments involves the critical analysis of an article; Unit 10 has been written to offer specific support for that task, although you will be aware that a careful and critical examination of the writings and activities of others permeates the whole course. Here I want first to raise some questions about the terms we use to discuss education and students, then to introduce some ideas for analysing the texts we read and write.

WATCHING WHAT WE SAY

5.7   Earlier in this unit I explained why I try to avoid talking of children *with special educational needs* or children *with* learning difficulties, because the terms are imprecise and imply deficiencies in students as the cause of difficulties in learning. This discomfort with terms is shared with others, however, though they may adopt different solutions. Referring to their book *Redefining the Whole Curriculum for Pupils with Learning Difficulties*, Judy Sebba, Richard Byers and Richard Rose (1993) argue:

> The text refers throughout to pupils with learning difficulties. We would have preferred to refer to 'pupils who are labelled as having ...' or 'pupils deemed to have ...' or some other phrase indicating the lottery nature of the system which leads to one pupil being given a label where another similar pupil has a different label or no label. In the interests of readability we have chosen the shorter version of 'pupils with learning difficulties'. However, we remain sceptical about the usefulness of this terminology. This leads us to keep reminding ourselves that labels are based on value judgements, which, however professional, may be misguided. It is an essential component of our position that the label should never be used to justify staff behaviour which threatens the dignity, rights or confidence of the pupils with whom we work.
>
> (Sebba, Byers and Rose, 1993, p. 4)

5.8   These authors did not consider the option of using the term 'students *who experience* difficulties in learning'. This might have led them to develop an approach to learning difficulties which includes learning for all.

5.9   But I try not to take my own concern over language too far. Colleagues at work talk of me as working on 'special needs' and while I find this mildly irritating, I do not waste my time, Canute-like, attempting to argue against the tide of their language.

5.10   Some of you may connect a concern with language to ideas about 'political correctness'. Jenny Corbett has made this link:

> New terms create discomfort and the political correctness of special education can become a tyranny. Some special educational needs coordinators in schools and colleges feel confused and anxious about changes in vocabulary, new systems and altered states. If they fail to adjust with sufficient speed and commitment they can begin to feel threatened and inadequate. This can build internal resentment and external conformity: an uneasy combination.
>
> (Corbett, 1993, p. 17)

5.11   The way to avoid a sense of discomfort with the expressions we use is to work out for ourselves how and why one wants to refer to school students, the difficulties they encounter and those who work with them. I do not find the notion of 'political correctness' or 'pc' useful. Generally it is used to refer to only one side of an argument. For example, those who use 'chair' or 'chairperson' to designate both men and women may be criticized for a concern with 'political correctness' while those whose politics leads them to refer to a woman as a 'chairman' are not seen to be so concerned. This does not make sense.

Activity 22   Naming the rose

Caroline Roaf describes herself as 'special needs co-ordinator' at Peers School in Oxfordshire. She has written about the way 'students' and student groupings are referred to at her school in Chapter 31 of Reader 1. She argues that the terms used to describe students and groupings, success and achievement, reflect and affect the way students are regarded in her school. Read her chapter carefully and consider your reactions to her suggestions. Do you agree that it is important to recognize and avoid the use of racist, sexist or disablist language or other words which devalue students in school? What terms does she suggest that we avoid? What should we put in their place? Does the use of terms assign differences in value to students? And is the assignment of differences in value a feature of school life that has to be accepted or even welcomed?

5.12   Caroline Roaf's chapter starts with her developing awareness of and acceptance of the need to avoid sexist and racist terms within her school as elsewhere. She accepts, for example, that referring to the active participants in the events of the world as if they are all men and boys can have real negative effects on the way people develop; that talking of skin colour as if it were all rosy pink can imply the invisibility of black students.

5.13   The use of discriminatory language is often, simply, rude. One woman headteacher referred to her experience on a panel interviewing six men and three women for a post of deputy head:

The county's training officer said, 'These are all potential deputy headmasters.' He was so insulting. I said, 'Excuse me, there is such a word as headteacher, could you please use it.' He was frightfully apologetic but it runs off the tongue so easily. How insulting it was to sit there as a female headteacher and hear the implication that the only person who could do the job was a man.

(Personal communication in Booth, 1987, p. xxiv)

5.14   Caroline Roaf, then, extends the argument to the use of other terms which she asserts 'imply differences in capabilities and worth'. Thus 'low ability', 'more able' and 'mixed ability' are to be avoided unless they refer 'to specific skills or talents'. No student is to be spoken of, or thought of, or responded to, as being generally more able or 'more intelligent' than any other student. She offers a challenge here to pervasive and deep-seated practices in schools and society. This is something that attitudes to ability share with approaches to 'race' and gender. Because racism and sexism pervade society it is argued that schools must have active anti-racist and anti-sexist policies in order to counter them. Do they also need anti-ablist and anti-disablist policies? It has become unfashionable to talk of class divisions in education. Whether this inattention reflects their removal from the structure of society or merely from the consciousness of writers on education will be considered in Unit 11/12.

5.15   At Whitmore, they have based their approach to preventing difficulties in learning on the development of 'mixed-ability teaching'. What does Caroline Roaf offer as a replacement term? Would 'balanced-group' teaching convey the same implications? It seems to lose the ideas that groups differ in attainment and in the way they might learn, though 'mixed-ability' may be a clumsy way of expressing these notions. What about 'heterogeneous group teaching'? The problem with introducing any new phrase is that it's difficult to find anyone who knows what you mean. I have opted to use 'mixed-attainment'.

5.16   The course's authors haven't conformed to Caroline Roaf's 'language of mutual respect' by referring consistently to children and young people who attend schools and colleges as students. Perhaps she means this to apply only to secondary students. But wouldn't such a difference reinforce status differences between primary and secondary schools and the teachers in them?

WRITING CLEARLY

5.17   A special language of 'special education' tends to perpetuate the separation of 'special' and 'mainstream' 'students' and 'teachers'. The expression of simple ideas using a professional language with its jargon and acronyms can be a way of avoiding exposing them to critical scrutiny as well as a means to create a professional chumminess.

Acronyms have exploded in number in education. The list of acronyms collected by the Libraries of Institutes and Schools of Education rose from 850 in 1981 to 3,000 in 1991 (Hutchinson, 1992). Within the latter list I found several double acronyms in which one letter stood for another acronym, and a triple acronym DELTA in which you have to know the meaning of two further acronyms before it makes even limited sense. (You may not wish to know that DELTA stands for Dissemination arising from Evaluation of Local TRIST Activities, TRIST stands for TVEI Related In-Service Training, and TVEI stands for the Technical and Vocational Educational Initiative – fortunately the DELTA project is now defunct.)

Activity 23   Gobbledygook or talking turkey?

In Reader 1, Chapter 32, Margaret Peter, editor of the *British Journal of Special Education,* has written about some of the unnecessary jargon she has encountered in surveying writing about education. Some of you may have tried to plough through impenetrable prose in an article in an educational journal, wondering why your capacity for understanding has suddenly become so deficient. Margaret Peter suggests that the fault is unlikely to be yours. As you read the chapter, consider whether your activities involve using language which excludes others from understanding them. Make a note of any parts of the chapter where you are expected to understand what is being said without sufficient information.

5.18   I feel that the message of this brief chapter is clear without further explanation from me. You may already find yourself enmeshed by the jargon of your workplace as part of a 'quality control service', for example, the new name for some LEA advisory and inspection services. You may not have the flexibility to resist jargon at work, so you can treat this course as an opportunity to escape from it – if we do our job properly.

5.19   Did you mind the echo of the beginning of *Pride and Prejudice* in the opening sentence? The return to Jane Austen with the final sentence of the chapter is neatly done but perhaps you find that literary allusions can be another way of excluding people. But it would be a pity to take this too far. We choose words in writing for a whole variety of conscious and unconscious reasons. They can fit their purpose well and have a more idiosyncratic derivation. The subtitle I added to the chapter you have just read, besides being an attempt to underline, in ironical fashion, the chapter's point, is also a reference to the work of Jurgen Habermas, about whom I know very little except for his suggestion that communication between people is most successful when it takes place in what he calls the 'ideal speech situation' where speakers have equal power. He is also renowned for the density of his prose. It is also a passing gentle acknowledgement to a friend, Heather Wood, who died while she was researching the applicability of the ideas of Habermas to special education. She felt that behind the complexities of expression were gems, not of ignorance, but brilliance.

READING CRITICALLY

5.20   It is reasonable to expect writers in education to express themselves clearly in language accessible to a wide audience. If we cannot understand what we read and we have good reason to suppose that we are included in the intended audience, then it is the writer's fault not ours. In Unit 10 I will set out an approach to critical reading in detail which you will need in order to do your fourth assignment. I will prepare you for the later work by introducing the concepts here. Some of you may be very familiar with this activity and so you can skim through this section and Unit 10 when you come to it so that you can compare your own approach with mine.

5.21   In making sense of educational documents such as articles in newspapers, professional and academic journals, government or governor or headteacher reports, it can be useful to take a systematic approach that pushes us to assess the piece of writing coolly and reflectively. This may be even more important when we want to redraft a piece of our own writing since it can be difficult to take a dispassionate look at our own carefully crafted creations.

5.22   I suggest that you develop your skills of critical reading using the following processes:

- distinguishing between *first reactions* and *subsequent readings* and between *style* and *content*;

- providing brief clear *summaries* of what you read;

- identifying the intended *audience* and the audience for whom the article is comprehensible and comparing the two;

- uncovering the *assumptions* the author makes about the knowledge, values and use of language that he or she shares with the reader;

- examining how *key terms* are defined and used;

- identifying the *assertions*, or claims to truth about the world, that are made and how these are linked together to form an *argument*;

- evaluating the *sense* of assertions, their *consistency* and the *contradictions* between them, and the *evidence* that is provided in support of them.

5.23   I will not develop these ideas in detail since that is the role of Unit 10, but I will introduce you to the tasks with an example.

Activity 24 Assumptions about disaffection

Consider the following introductory paragraph taken from a chapter entitled 'Overcoming passive disaffection: students with severe physical disability', contributed by David Hutchinson, to a book entitled *Uneasy Transitions: disaffection in post-compulsory education and training*.

> Disaffection can take many forms and it may be considered strange to suggest that students with severe physical disability might show but the remotest symptom of it. However, if one takes the view that disaffection in education might be any behavioural factor that prevents positive learning taking place, then it can be argued that this student group can show every bit as much disaffection as can any other student group. In this case however, the disaffection is not of an aggressive nature, indeed, the opposite is very much the case. I shall call this type of disaffection *passive* and the ensuing chapter will describe approaches which have been developed by one college of further education in an attempt to overcome it.
>
> (Hutchinson, 1990, p. 56)

- What are the main assertions in this paragraph?

- How is disaffection defined and how does this compare with the definition in paragraph 1.17 of this unit?

- What assumptions are made about how the reader will view disaffection at the start of the paragraph and the possibility of students with severe disabilities being disaffected?

5.24   There are a number of claims made in this paragraph but I take the main assertions to be:

1   Disaffection can take many forms.

2   Students with severe disabilities are as likely to be disaffected as students without disabilities.

3   Students with severe disabilities express disaffection passively.

5.25   You may feel that the first of these is a little trivial to be classed as 'main'. However, I get the impression that the author thinks that he is imparting information by telling us this.

5.26   The author defines disaffection in terms of behaviour whereas I defined it in terms of feelings of dissatisfaction, rejection, and opposition. The author's definition may include too much. A garrulous, cheerful sociability might interfere with learning but would we or the author want to call it disaffection?

5.27   The author *assumes* that we will think of disaffection as an aggressive response to education. He thinks we *assume* that severely disabled students cannot be aggressively disaffected. Therefore, he thinks that we may consider it strange to think of severely disabled students as disaffected. I cannot tell whether his assumptions were correct for you but I find them a little 'strange' themselves. Did you think of disaffection only as aggressive actions? Why shouldn't disabled students display aggression?

5.28 Later in the chapter, Hutchinson says of 'young people with severe disabilities': 'I would stress that such young people should not be seen as a homogeneous group but as unique individuals with many differences'. This would seem to *contradict* the earlier view that as a group they do not display disaffection as aggression.

5.29 Many disabled people would object to the way Hutchinson refers to 'young people *with* severe disabilities', wishing to claim their disability as essential to their identity by the phrase 'disabled people'. Disabled people also express their dissatisfaction with services, laws and the way they are represented by the media and through charity advertising in active and angry ways. This is *evidence* against Hutchinson's views. If you read the rest of his chapter you will be able to assess the evidence he provides.

CONCLUDING REMARK

5.30 In this section I have discussed the language of respect, the use and avoidance of jargon, and an approach to critical reading. We have made the tasks of critical reading explicit in this course because we have found that some people on previous courses have difficulty in challenging the authority of the printed word. We also found that some students would end their studies without subjecting their own views to examination and at least refining the justifications for them. If at the end of this course you think and act in the same way and with the same set of justifications as you did at the start then we will have failed.

6   INVESTIGATIONS

6.1 All the units in the course end with a discussion of topics for further investigation. We want you to identify and follow up your own interests and you will have to include one investigation in your assignments. In this unit I have suggested that you begin to identify aspects of education in your own local area that you would like to know more about. Towards the end of the next unit we will consider basic approaches to research, particularly observation and interviewing, which may help you to carry out an investigation. The research we wish to foster through this course starts from an interest in asking a question about something to which you do not yet have an answer.

6.2 In my study of the Grove school I discussed how an examination of one aspect of the education system can lead to an analysis of a wide range of educational concerns. I have started to discuss a considerable number of topics throughout the unit, each one of which could form the basis for several assignment-length studies.

6.3 What you can choose for further local study will depend, among other things, on your job, your family, acquaintances and involvement in education and the use you make of the resources available to you such as the other students on this course. Are you a school governor? Can you join a school trip? Do you know a traveller who would chat to you about their way of life at home and at school? Do you know parents of children or young people with disabilities? Besides using an investigation to find the answer to a question about education that has been puzzling you, you can also use it to check assertions or compare with reports of experiences in the units.

6.4 I have set out a few examples below. In any investigation you will have to think carefully about issues of confidentiality.

When and why is learning difficult?

6.5 Ask students at varying stages in the education system to identify any difficulties faced in school, now and in the past, for themselves and for their friends. Compare their view of education with your own memories of school and compare these with the perspectives of school workers. Do you or any of your acquaintances work in a school? What makes life difficult for school workers? It might help to try to systematize your enquiries by picking a particular school day and asking your informants to take you through the difficulties encountered.

Care and education

6.6 Can you visit a children's home and discuss perceptions of education with willing members of staff and children and young people? Your local social services department might be able to help you if you contact them and explain your purpose. You would need to think out carefully what you might want to ask of the workers and children in the home. What do the workers know about the education of the children and young people in their care? What experiences do the young people have of school?

The story of a statement

6.7 Do you know a parent of a child who is the subject of a statement or record? What has been their experience of the statementing process? Look at the process of compiling the statement, the sense and usefulness of the reports and advice it contains. How do teachers contribute to and regard the process?

A school trip

6.8   What preparation do the pupils have for the trip? What are they expected to gain from it? What presents difficulties for them? How is the content of the trip integrated into lessons at school?

Inclusion and exclusion?

6.9   What is the range of pupils included at a particular school? Who, from the community which surrounds the school, is excluded? What are the grounds for exclusion?

How and why are students grouped?

6.10   How do the teachers in a primary or secondary school group the students they teach for different activities? What is the rationale behind the grouping? What do students understand about the reasons for groupings and what do they think of them?

APPENDIX 1   WHO'S TO BLAME? A MULTI-LAYERED EPIC

Dennis Mongon and Susan Hart

> … any incident is a climax or crisis in a number of 'stories'. Both pupils and teachers carry their stories with them into school, the clash of stories makes a multi-layered epic.
>
> (Shostak, 1983, p. 113)

1   THE CAST

Mary: The second-in-charge of the school's on-site 'disruptive unit'
Fred: The excluded pupil
Sheila: A history teacher involved in the incident
Carol: The culprit

2   THE SCENE

The summer term is drawing to a close and the atmosphere at Pilgrim's Way is becoming increasingly festive and frenetic. The ritual end-of-year activities – sports days, concerts, day trips, parents' evenings, reports, prize days, fêtes, concerts and plays – are all taking their toll, while teachers struggle to find the extra energy to attend to the final details of next year's timetable, option lists, tutor groups, teaching rooms, planning of new courses, ordering and printing of materials and preparations for the new intake for the coming September. In the midst of it all, of course, teaching is expected to go on as usual.

3 MARY'S STORY

Mary has been working with Fred in the school's disruptive unit for some time and is feeling optimistic about the possibility of his successful reintegration into lessons. However, her day begins not with thoughts of Fred, but with another pupil who has been truanting. She has been asked to call for him at home and bring him into school.

8.00 a.m.

Today I have to leave early to collect a school refuser from his home. I hope that this will enable him to settle into coming to school on a more regular basis. However, listening to the weather forecast, it looks like it will mean me getting and staying wet for half an hour longer than usual.

8.30 a.m.

The steady drizzle turns into rain, and as I arrive at the house I am met by a rather large dog wagging its tail and baring its teeth at the same time. Jack's brother opens the door and the dog goes in, but it is obvious that I'm not going to be let over the doorstep. All manner of strange noises come from within the house, including the sound of Jack trying to fight whoever is using forceful persuasion to get him to come and meet me. Eventually, amidst much cursing from the upstairs of the house, Jack appears and we start the journey to school. Little conversation happens on the way because Jack refuses to talk to me. I can't say I blame him. I feel that I have intruded on his privacy.

9.00 a.m.

We arrive safely in the unit. I had taken Jack to see his year head before registration period so that they could become reacquainted. This was a partial success. It seemed that the year head was biting her tongue over something that had happened in the past but was desperately trying to appear as if she was pleased to see him. I didn't witness the whole of the interview because I had to go and remind the head of fourth year about another pupil from the unit who had been out of humanities for two months and is due back to lessons today. On the way back to the year head's office, I bumped into Fred himself and reminded him about going to humanities. He appeared relaxed because they were going to watch a video. His manner confirmed my feeling that he would be all right in lessons from now on. He had made significant progress in managing his own behaviour, or perhaps he had just grown up. When I finally returned to collect Jack, he had a slight smile on his face. The year head looked decidedly grey.

9.15 a.m.

Teaching for the morning under way. Two children are doing maths, one reading, one English, one humanities and two are setting up the computer instead of doing French. I am trying to fill in some admittance details with Jack. After doing this, which takes rather a long time because I keep having to answer questions about which lead goes where on the computer and what a maths problem really means, the first double period has nearly gone and it is time for break.

10.15 a.m.

Break time. Take Jack back into school explaining that he has now got to go back to his lessons for the morning because I am support teaching next lesson, and after that I am teaching my own English group. He gives me a slight smile, only the second time I've seen it today, and makes off towards some friends of his. I go in search of a cup of tea.

10.35 a.m.

Support teaching with a second year group, perhaps the most enjoyable session of the week. I'm supporting this group in lessons because it has three unit pupils in it, and potentially more on the way. It has always struck me that many of the pupils I see in the unit would be better dealt with in their tutor groups and through adaptations to the curriculum presented to them. It can be a very enjoyable experience producing new work for the group and seeing it going down well. And there are always lessons to be learned from seeing it fail miserably! The lesson today is a success. The children work well in their groups and appear engrossed.

1.00 pm

A fairly normal morning. Not so the lunch hour! All interest in my salad roll evaporates when Fred's humanities teacher comes up and tells me she has had a bad time in the lesson with Fred. Apparently, she sent him to the year head for swearing at her. I don't believe Fred could have reacted like this without provocation. It transpires that he was accused of stealing some money by one of the girls in the group and it grew from there. I set off in search of the year head, and after ten minutes spent scouring the building, discover him back in the staffroom telling jokes. He tells me in an off-hand way that the head has decided to exclude Fred for leaving school premises without permission and for using threatening and abusive language to a member of staff. I feel extremely irritated that nobody has bothered to inform me, let alone ask me how the situation should be handled. It is two hours since the head made that decision, but no note or communication from anyone to me. The year head's reaction is that we are all better off without Fred; he's taken up more than his fair share of everyone's time and patience already, and deserves all he gets. He turns back to tell the next joke.

1.45 pm

I catch up with head, who confirms to me that Fred has been excluded because she has had enough of him. I try to point out that several good things have been happening with him as well, but the matter is already closed. The head is more interested in telling me about a meeting next week which appears to mean that there are going to be larger first-year groups next year because of falling rolls, and that we can have no in-service education time for special needs next year because the fourth- and fifth-year curricula have priority. I try to argue that working with an advisory teacher on classroom management will eventually be of benefit to the fourth and fifth years. In return, I receive a speech about who has to carry the can.

1.55 pm

I go back to the staff room feeling very disillusioned with life and find a note in my pigeon hole telling me that Jack did not turn up for his lesson after break. There is no time to do anything about that now. I suppose I will be back on his doorstep tomorrow morning. I leave the staff room thinking that I have one of two choices, getting muddy going back to the unit in the rain or following my pupil's example and going home quietly without telling anyone. I choose the mud only because I'm not as brave as he is.

4 FRED'S STORY

Fred is fourteen years old. He is a fourth-year pupil, and has a long history of difficult, disruptive behaviour stretching back to his primary school days. His teachers have 'tried everything' with him, but apparently to no avail. He seems to have difficulty in grasping what it is about his behaviour that the school finds so objectionable, and feels that he is victimized by teachers because they regard him as a trouble-maker. He looks back on the incident that got him excluded and expresses, with some bitterness, his feelings about it.

My name's Fred and this is my story, although you probably won't believe me. Nobody ever does. I've been at this school for nearly four years now and really, I quite like it. No, not the lessons (I think they're boring), but I like coming to see my mates.

When I was in the first year, they sent me to see a psychologist. I don't think they wanted me at this school, but I said I wanted to stay and he said that I could. Since then things have been all right. I've been kicked out a few times – you know – excluded, but they were for things that weren't my fault. Once you've got a face, you get picked on. Like there was this time when I was fooling around with my mates in the gym. We'd asked to go to the toilet during the maths lesson and the teacher let us. Anyway, we found this tennis ball in the gym which was on the way to the toilet, and we were kicking it around, when it hit the fire alarm and the alarm went off. I got three days out for that. Nobody else did. Something about it being their first offence. It just goes to show that once you've got a face, they'll do you.

I'm supposed to be telling you what happened yesterday. The school has got this unit, and I've been in and out of there for the last few years. It's where they send you when your subject teacher has got fed up with you. I've been in there for science because they said I was dangerous. I ask you! And just recently I've been in there for humanities. I don't know why that was, but it gave me a chance to catch up on me homework and the work in class. Last week, the teacher says to me 'Do you think you are ready to go back to the lesson?' I says 'Yes'. Anyway, they were going to have this video next lesson so I agree to go back. Just before registration, the teacher from the unit saw me and told me to be a good boy and all that stuff. I said I would, 'cause it was the video, see. I went off to register, but I didn't stay in the room because I've got mates all over the school, and it is one of the times of the day that you can see them.

I got to the lesson and everything seemed to be OK. The teacher was in a bit of a huff, but that was because she was late setting up, and there was this girl surrounded by other girls. There was a lot of chattering and the girl in the middle was crying. The teacher went over to them. I suppose she had no choice really, but I bet she thought it was a pain in the neck, first lesson and all that. Then suddenly out of the blue she comes over to me and asks if I was out of my tutor room this morning. I said 'Yes', because I'd been out seeing my mates. Then she tells me in this really snooty voice that some money has gone missing from one of the lockers, £10 to be precise. She asks me again what I was doing out of my tutor room. I've already answered that question, so I guessed she was accusing me of taking it. Well, I'm not having that. I might be a face, but I'm no thief, so I told her where to get off. We had this slanging match, and she told me to get out and go to Mr Hardaway. Fat chance of me going anywhere near him. I decided to go home and let them all cool off.

Anyway, this morning my mum got this letter telling her I'd been excluded until further notice, not because I'd stolen the money – I hadn't, so they can't do me for that – but because I'd used bad language to a teacher. Honestly, who's ever heard of anybody being excluded for swearing when they've been wrongly accused of theft?

You ought to hear some of the teachers' language! It goes to show that if you've got a face, they'll do you in the end.

5 SHEILA'S STORY

Sheila is an experienced history teacher. She is also a tutor of a third-year class and takes her pastoral responsibilities seriously, although there is never enough time. Today turns out to be one of these days when the pressure gets too much ...

8.30 a.m.

There's a cover slip with my name on it lurking by the head's daily notices and I discover that I have won the dubious privilege of an hour's drama with 3L last thing this afternoon in the year base immediately facing the head's office. I'm just getting accustomed to that thrill in prospect, when Lyn, my class's geography teacher, comes beaming into my field of vision. I feel my defences rising. I know when she looks like that it means my class has been playing up again (and somehow there's always a sense that it's a reflection on the tutor when a class is badly behaved). It turns out that she's given the whole class a detention, which she knows is officially against school policy, but she couldn't sort out who the ring leaders were and they drove her to the point where she couldn't think what else to do. She wants to come into my registration period this morning and warn them in front of me to be sure to turn up. (Her confidence in the deterrent effects of my influence is gratifying but, I fear, ill-founded.)

The first pips go as she speaks, and everyone starts pushing past us towards the door. I should be going too, of course, but I can't exactly abandon Lyn in mid-sentence, so I avoid noticing the deputy head in charge of registers who is trying to attract my attention by waving my register in the air. I feel a bit awkward because I want to help but I know that if she comes straight in with me now it will look to my class like I'm taking her side without listening to their point of view. I stall for time to think by asking her to tell me exactly what they were getting up to in her lesson. At the same time, I'm uncomfortably aware of my deputy head's increasingly frenzied gesticulations in my direction.

The scene Lyn describes is all too painfully familiar, but if it was me I couldn't be quite so sure that it was only the kids who were at fault. Still, it's not my place to say so, and anyway if I try to hold out a moment longer I think the unfortunate deputy head might become locked into permanent spasm. Moving backwards towards the door, I suggest we leave it until tomorrow. She agrees, somewhat reluctantly, and I escape down the corridor. It's a nuisance because I've already got more than enough things to get through in my tutor period today. There's Sukhjit and Helen for one thing. I've been trying to find time to talk to them about homework for days. I suspect that they've got nowhere quiet to work at home, and I might be able to get some arrangement made for them at school. I also intended to get the journals signed up to date this morning. The familiar sense of too much to do and too little time to do it is beginning to build up again. It takes another surge forward as, half-way to my tutor room, I remember I haven't got the video I need for my first lesson. Oh well, I'll have to collect it from the faculty room after registration.

8.50 a.m.

'Late detention for you, Miss!' my kids heckle self-righteously as I scurry towards the tutor room. They pile through the door and I'm grateful that for once they seem prepared to settle down quite calmly. I decide to ignore surreptitious chewing and non-regulation attire for once – much to the annoyance, no doubt, of those who were angling to get sent home to change. There's a limit to what you can tackle constructively at any one time, and I need to keep the atmosphere positive for the discussion to follow.

After the register, I tell them all to bring their chairs into a circle round my desk, and in my best pastoral manner to try to open up a responsible discussion about the problem in geography. The response is predictable, if disappointing. Their faces assume that familiar expression of wide-eyed innocence which they've perfected over years of experience of dealing with such situations. Then they launch into a tirade about how boring the lesson is and how moany the teacher is etc., which is highly embarrassing and exactly what I don't want to happen. I try to steer them off that and get them to consider what they could do themselves to improve the situation, but they just look blank as if they don't see that it's up to them. I find myself saying things like: 'Just because you don't like a lesson, it does not give you the right to be rude or to stop other people from learning', but they don't look any more convinced than I feel. I try not to show it, of course, but underneath I wonder if it isn't more worrying if children *don't* act up when they're bored, but just sit there compliantly and take whatever is meted out to them. I am at a loss to know how to bring the 'discussion' to a constructive conclusion, but the pips solve that for me. I wonder if anything has been achieved by this small foray into pupil participation and democracy. I have my doubts.

Just as they're all bundling off towards the door, glad to escape, no doubt, I remember the notice about lining up for dinners that I'm supposed to have read out to them. I can imagine the chaos (and complaints from colleagues on dinner duty) if my class don't know what the new arrangements are, so I frantically call them all back and make them write the information down in their journals, fending off the groans and complaints as good humouredly as I can manage as the minutes tick relentlessly on. By the time they've finished, the second years due to come into the room have already started arriving outside and are falling over each other trying to press their noses against the glass panel of the door. They think it's a huge joke to hold on to the door handle so that my class can't get out. I issue a few threats and manage to wrench the door open, and then, of course, both lots of children push forward simultaneously so that the sea of bodies presses itself to a standstill. I yell at them to use their common sense, and expend more energy restoring them to some semblance of order before I can make my getaway. I finally head off down the corridor already more than five minutes late for my lesson.

9.12 a.m.

Today being one of those days, my lateness does not, of course, go unobserved. Rounding the final bend, I spy, with sinking spirits, yet another of the ubiquitous senior staff in the process of subduing my fourth year history group outside my teaching room. She looks pointedly at her watch as I scramble up the corridor, still clutching the register which both she and I know should by now have been sent to the general office. I mutter my apologies to her supercilious departing back, remembering I still haven't collected the video that I need to start the lesson.

I'm beginning to feel like I've done a day's work already. The fourth years seem to be pretty 'high', too. Maybe it's only because I'm late. I decide to give us all a chance to calm down, and just mark the names quietly in the register instead of calling them out as I usually do. Fred's back, I see. I wonder if he's the reason for the mood they're in. He always used to have a bad effect on them when he was there before, but he hasn't been in my lessons for a while because he's been going to the unit. I wonder if I should choose him to go down to the faculty room for the video. The others might settle down better without him there, and it might give him a chance to start again on a positive note. I decide not to risk it. He might not feel like doing me any favours yet.

There's a commotion going on in one corner. Sacha is in tears and her friends are fussing round her trying to comfort her. I don't relish the thoughts of sorting out another problem, but no work is going to get done unless I do. I take a deep breath and go over to the group.

Apparently someone has taken her school-journey money from her locker during registration. They say they think it was Fred because he was wandering about the school. I turn to Fred, and before I know what's happening, he starts shouting and swearing at me. The shock of his reaction makes me flip my lid too and before I can stop myself I've told him to get out and report to the year head. As soon as I've said it, I wish I hadn't, because, of course, he just sits there refusing to budge and I've got another problem on my hands about how to make him go short of using physical force (and he's bigger than me, anyway). He stares at me threateningly for what seems like hours, and I'm panicking inside wondering if there's any way I can give in gracefully without losing face with the other children. Just as I'm thinking I'll have to do something, he gets up and slams out of the room with a gesture of defiance in my direction which leaves no one in any doubts as to what he thinks of me.

The relief I feel at his departure is more than compensation, but I'm shaking inside too. It really upsets me to have a confrontation with a kid. Deep down, I'm on their side, but that's not the way they see you. It's so hard to strike the right balance with some of them. If you're nice, they think you're soft. If you're not, they treat you like the enemy. I wish I'd been more careful with Fred, but he just caught me off my guard. I really wasn't accusing him of stealing the money; he just chose to take it that way. And I had to react to him swearing at me. School policy is if they swear at staff, they're out – all the kids know it. I'll go and see the year head at break and explain what happened. Except I'm on duty, so I'll have to settle for a note instead.

The rest of the class are a bit shocked and hushed after Fred's departure. Should I talk to them about the incident or not? I really can't face it, or the video for that matter. I feel completely drained. Better for all of us to escape behind an anonymous worksheet until the pips go to release us.

1.00 pm

I've been so busy for the rest of the morning that I haven't had time to think about Fred again until now. I wonder if the year head got my note. The unit teacher is in the staff room eating her sandwiches and I talk to her about the incident. She hadn't heard about it. In fact, she's very upset and I can quite see why. She's spent a lot of time working with Fred, and now she feels it's all been wasted. She rushes straight off to find the year head, and I feel even worse.

4.00 pm

I've just heard that Fred was excluded because of the incident with me. It turns out that he never reported to the year head (surprise, surprise), but just ran out of school. The head said it was the last straw, that he'd had all the chances it was reasonable to give, not to mention costly one-to-one individual support in the unit. She said you had to draw the line somewhere. I tried to explain that the incident had been partly my fault, but she didn't want to know, nor did the year head. I've got a feeling they're both glad to see the back of him. But I'm left with a terrible sense of guilt.

Carol is fifteen years old and a pupil in Sheila's fourth-year history group. She rarely gets into trouble because she is always one step ahead of everyone else. She appears to have no scruples whatsoever about the money she has stolen, and takes great delight in watching the incident with Fred, enjoying the sense of power she gets from being the one in the know.

It's been a right laugh in history today. Quite a little *drama*. I could tell Miss was over the top the minute she appeared. Must have got out of bed the wrong side. You'd think that would be a warning to the rest of them to keep their heads down, but not the boys, oh no!

If you ask me, Fred had it coming to him. You'd have thought Fred would have learnt by now that the best thing to do when anyone tries to pin anything on you is to stay cool, look them straight in the eye and deny it. You can be sure I had my excuses ready if anyone happened to inquire how come I'd got ten quid on me when a ten pound note had just done a disappearing trick. But I don't think I'll be needing them now after the way Fred carried on.

You've got to beat teachers at their own game. It's no good looking for trouble, because they'll always get you in the end. You have to pretend to do all the things they want you to do. They love that. Some kids just can't help smirking and shrugging their shoulders when they get told off, to show they don't care. That really gets teachers going. You should watch me and my mate Alison. We can stop just about any teacher in their tracks, no matter what we've done. What you do is: you *smile*, you *apologize*, and you *look as if you mean it*. Magic.

Getting done for swearing is too stupid. Still, it's even more stupid the way these teachers act so touchy when anyone swears, as though it offends their sensitive ears. They must hear people saying the same words every day outside of school and they can't send *them* to the year head. I sometimes wonder how these high-and-mighty teachers manage outside of school, when they can't order people around and give them detentions to make them do what they want.

Anyway, the excitement's over. Fred's gone and Miss looks like she's about to burst into tears. She's handed us this mind-blowingly boring worksheet and told us to get on with it, and now she's sat at her desk with her head in her hands like a silent movie. Well, I'm not about to waste my time doing some stupid questions when she's being paid to teach us. They go on and on about how important our 'education' is, and this is what we get! Out of the window, I can see the second years clodhopping it round the netball pitch, but it's more than my delicate eyes can stand. I nudge my mate to pass me the magazine she's reading under the desk. She doesn't want to, but she's hoping to get a share in the takings so she can't ignore me. I flip through the pages until the pips go. Some education!

(Mongon *et al.*, 1989, pp. 9–20)

APPENDIX 2   THE OPEN-AIR SCHOOL: SUNSHINE, REST AND FOOD

If the Open Air School on the Milton Road at Cambridge is a special school, it is that the children attending there may have a health giving environment – with fresh air, rest and proper food guaranteed. What these children have, all children should have, and the ordinary school functions on the basis that they do have them and concentrates on the things of the mind until physical ills obtrude. The home environment may have been healthy, but the children are deficient, most of them deficient in body, some deficient in mind. Little bodies are strengthened, handicapped intelligences are stimulated.

A SYMBOLIC FENCE

There is a fence at the Open Air School which is symbolic of the rigid division between the two departments. For the backward minds there is a special curriculum, and each child receives more individual attention than is possible in an ordinary primary school, because more guidance is necessary. Psychology is doing its beneficent work. Most of these children are strong in body, and they do not require the special feeding. They have the mid-day meal at the school, but not breakfast and tea. Hand-work has an important place in their instruction, and the school equipment will not be complete until even better provision than at present is made for it. At least that was the impression made on the writer of this article when he visited the school with the Medical Officer of Health. Larger rooms for domestic instruction and for manual training will be required, for in this department the permanent structures have had to be supplemented by temporary buildings. For the children whose minds are struggling towards the light the classes are smaller than on the other side of the school – twenty-five as compared with forty. All teaching is exacting for the teacher, but here patience works miracles among the seventy children who would be handicapped in their own age groups at an ordinary school. There is a feeling of buoyant hopefulness. The work is but beginning, and in that fact alone there is tremendous encouragement. Children are not being left in darkness to struggle unaided, in an environment which is bound to beat them.

PREVENTION

Very different is the problem among the children whose growing bodies need care, and the task of the school is simpler. Minds are bright, but physical strength must not be overtaxed or must be built up. There are 120 and over 96 hangs the cloud of the possibility of tuberculosis. Eighty per cent of them have been sent to the school by the Tuberculosis Officer for the County, Dr Paton Philip, and the headteacher and the Schools Medical Officer work in combination to prevent a favourable field for the growth of the dreaded germ. The Open Air School is fighting to keep the population of Papworth Village Settlement down. It is part of the machinery of the community warring against consumption.

There is a good deal of the atmosphere of the hospital about the school. At its centre is the Medical Officer's room where the pupils, or the patients – as you like – are examined weekly. The medical history of each is carefully docketed and every increase in weight is noted as something gained, while a fall is a matter for anxious consideration. Personal hygiene is inculcated as of supreme importance, and to realize that it is only necessary to walk into the lavatory, which is something very different to the normal washing place of an ordinary primary school at present. There are the tumbler, tooth brush, hair brush, and comb in a bag for each child, in racks round the walls, and the set of each is a strictly personal thing identified by a number. The washing basins, fitted with hot and cold water taps, in number and cleanliness as such as each school should obtain. There are shower baths in the bath room with the temperature of the water controlled. A trained nurse superintends the cult of the body.

FOOD

The kitchen, too, occupies a commanding place in the school equipment, and the cook and her staff serve three meals a day – breakfast, dinner and tea. The dietary table has a scientific foundation, for it is framed by the Medical Officer, the food is perfectly prepared in a well-equipped kitchen, and it is served in a dining room that encourages appetite. The children are not consulted as to the food placed before them and they eat everything with the complete enjoyment proper to youngsters. The school garden supplies the kitchen with vegetables, and an orchard of young trees is yielding fruit. Milk, butter and eggs are sent direct to the school. Payment of five shillings a week covers the full cost of the food consumed by each child, and when they are able to do so parents contribute that amount. The scale of contribution is based upon a formula, which ensures the cost to the ratepayers is as small as possible. The full contribution is being paid for 75 per cent of the children.

When the children arrive at the school in the morning by omnibus, they divest themselves of their clothing and dress in garments suitable for the season that the sun may do its beneficent work upon their bodies. In the summer time the boys wear cotton slips and they are bare above the waist. The girls have knickers and tunics of cotton. In the cold weather big woollen sweaters are worn. With tanned skins the youngsters do not feel the cold as do their brothers and sisters, whose bodies are not constantly exposed to sun and air.

EPIDEMICS AVOIDED

The midday rest which is imperative in the school is in the open air, and the children are never cold. In wet weather the canvas beds are ranged in open sheds and in winter the children are tucked up in blankets, and each child has his or her own blanket. The classrooms are screened with glass, but the screens are not used without cause, and even when fully screened there is free play for the air above the screens. The result is that epidemics of colds do not sweep through the school, and there has been a 90 per cent attendance in the present year, while the percentage for the whole of last year was 89. In the upper room there was an attendance of 95 per cent.

The period at which a child is at the school varies considerably. Some children are there for a few weeks and return to the ordinary primary school. Others are there for two or three years. It is used as a place of recuperation. All the schools of the future will be open-air schools. The new infant schools planned for Romsey Town and Chesterton will contain many of the ideas of this school, which was designed by the Borough Surveyor after fourteen years of consideration and investigation by the Education Committee. It began in 1914 owing to the public-spirited generosity of Mrs Alan Gray, who placed in the hands of the Committee the means of starting a class at Vinery Road. After the war it was some years before the Town Council could persuade the Board of Education to sanction the expenditure. To get the authorisation required persistent effort, and it was at length obtained when Lord Eustace Percy and the late Sir Geoffrey Butler were together for an hour or two in a railway carriage. The school was opened in May, 1927.
(*Cambridge Chronicle and University Journal*, 8 October 1930, p. 9)

REFERENCES

ACKER, S. (1989) *Teachers, Gender and Careers*, London, Falmer Press.

ADES, A., PARKER, S., BERRY, T., HOLLAND, F., DAVISON, C., CUBITT, D., HJELM, M., WILCOX, A., HUDSON, C., BRIGGS, M., TEDDER, R. and PECKAM, C. (1991)

'Prevalence of maternal HIV1 infection in Thames Regions: results from anonymous unlinked neonatal testing', *The Lancet*, **337**(8757), pp. 1562–5.

ALLAN, J., BROWN, S. AND MUNN, P. (1991) *Off the Record: mainstream provision for pupils with non-recorded learning difficulties in primary and secondary schools*, Edinburgh, Scottish Centre for Research in Education.

BINNS, D. (1984) *Children's Literature and the Role of the Gypsy*, Manchester, Traveller Education Service.

BINNS, D. (1990) 'History and growth of traveller education', *British Journal of Educational Studies*, **38**(3), pp. 251–8.

BOOTH, T. (1987) 'Introduction' in BOOTH, T. and COULBY, D. (eds) *Producing and Reducing Disaffection*, Milton Keynes, Open University Press/The Open University.

BOOTH, T. and COULBY, D. (eds) (1987) *Producing and Reducing Disaffection*, Milton Keynes, Open University Press/The Open University.

BOOTH, T. and STATHAM, J. (1982) 'William: a child with Down's syndrome' in BOOTH, T. and STATHAM, J. (eds) *The Nature of Special Education*, London, Croom Helm/The Open University.

BOOTH, T. and SWANN, W. (eds) (1987) *Including Pupils with Disabilities*, Milton Keynes, Open University Press/The Open University.

BOOTH, T., POTTS, P., and SWANN, W. (eds) (1987) *Preventing Difficulties in Learning*, Oxford, Basil Blackwell/The Open University.

BROWN, S. (1994) 'The Scottish national curriculum and special educational needs', *The Curriculum Journal*, **5**(1), pp. 83–94.

CHIN, J. (1990) 'Current and future dimensions of the HIV/AIDS pandemic in women and children', *The Lancet*, **336**(8708), pp. 134–6.

CORBETT, J. (1993) 'Special language and political correctness', *British Journal of Special Education*, **21**(1), pp. 17–19.

DE LYON, H. and WIDDOWSON-MIGNIUOLO, F. (1989) *Women Teachers: issues and experiences*, Milton Keynes, Open University Press.

DEPARTMENT FOR EDUCATION (DFE) (1994) *Code of Practice on the Identification and Assessment of Special Educational Needs,* London, Department for Education.

DEPARTMENT FOR EDUCATION (DFE) (1995) *The National Curriculum*, London, DFE.

DEPARTMENT OF EDUCATION AND SCIENCE (DES) (1978) *Special Educational Needs*, Report of the Committee of Enquiry into the Education of Handicapped Children and Young People, London, HMSO (the Warnock Report).

DEPARTMENT OF EDUCATION AND SCIENCE (DES) (1985a) *Education for All*, London, HMSO (the Swann Report).

DEPARTMENT OF EDUCATION AND SCIENCE (DES) (1985b) *The Education of Travellers' Children: an HMI discussion paper*, London, HMSO.

DEPARTMENT OF EDUCATION AND SCIENCE (DES) (1989) *A Survey of Support Services for Special Educational Needs*, London, HMSO (Report by HM Inspectors).

DESSENT, T. (1987) *Making the Ordinary School Special*, Lewes, Falmer Press.

DOYLE, C. (1989) *Working with Abused Children*, London, Macmillan.

EGGLESTON, J., DUNN, D., ANJALI, M. and WRIGHT, C. (1985) *The Educational and Vocational Experiences of 15–18-year-old Members of Minority Ethnic Groups*, Stoke-on-Trent, Trentham Books.

EUROPEAN COLLABORATIVE STUDY (1991) 'Children born to women with HIV-1 infection: natural history and risk of transmission', *The Lancet*, **337**(8736), pp. 253–60.

FLETCHER-CAMPBELL, F. and HALL, C. L. (1990) *Changing Schools? Changing People? A study of the education of children in care*, Slough, NFER.

FLEW, A. (1990) 'A code of malpractice?', *Times Educational Supplement*, 2 March 1990, p. 23.

FORDYCE, W. (1987) 'A policy for Grampian' in BOOTH, T., POTTS, P. and SWANN, W. (eds) (1987) *Preventing Difficulties in Learning*, Oxford, Basil Blackwell/The Open University.

GILBERT, C., and HART, M. (1990) *Towards Integration: special needs in an ordinary school*, London, Kogan Page.

GILBORN, D. (1990) *'Race', Ethnicity and Education: teaching and learning in multi-ethnic schools*, London, Unwin Hyman.

GIPPS, C., GROSS, H. and GOLDSTEIN, H. (1987) *Warnock's Eighteen Per Cent*, Lewes, Falmer Press.

HARDY, T. (1872) *Under the Greenwood Tree*, published in paperback by Macmillan, 1974.

HERBERT, C. (1989) *Talking of Silence: the sexual harassment of schoolgirls*, London, Falmer Press.

HULL, R. (1985) *The Language Gap*, London, Methuen.

HUTCHINSON, D. (1990) 'Overcoming passive disaffection: students with severe physical disability' in CORBETT, J. (ed.) *Uneasy Transitions: disaffection in post-compulsory education and training*, London, Falmer Press.

HUTCHINSON, J. (1992) *Acronyms and Initialisms in Education, a handlist*, Libraries of Institutes and Schools of Education, University of East Anglia.

IVATTS, A. (1975) *Catch 22 Gypsies*, London, Advisory Committee for the Education of Romany and Other Travellers.

JONES, C. (1985) 'Sexual tyranny: male violence in a mixed secondary school', in WEINER, G. (ed.) *Just a Bunch of Girls*, Milton Keynes, Open University Press.

KAHAN, B. (1979) *Growing up in Care*, Oxford, Blackwell.

KAHAN, B. (1994) *Growing up in Groups*, London, HMSO.

KAHAN, B. and LEVY, A. (1991) *The Report of the Staffordshire Child Care Inquiry*, Staffordshire County Council.

KAVANAGH, P. J. and MICHIE, J. (eds) (1985) *The Oxford Book of Short Poems*, Oxford, Oxford University Press.

KENRICK, D. and BAKEWELL, S. (1990) *On the Verge: the gypsies of England*, London, The Runnymede Trust.

THE LANCET (1991) Editorial: 'Anonymous HIV testing: latest results', *The Lancet*, **337**(8757), pp. 1572–3.

LEE, C. (1990) 'Natural history of HIV and AIDS', *AIDS Care*, **2**(4) pp. 353–7.

LIÉGEOIS, J. P. (1987) *School Provision for Gypsy and Traveller Children*, Luxembourg, Office for Official Publications of the European Communities.

MACDONALD, I., BHARNARI, R., KHAN, L. and JOHN, G. (1989) *Murder in the Playground: the report of the Macdonald Inquiry into racism and racial violence in Manchester schools*, London, Longsight Press.

MAHER, P. (ed.) (1987) *Child Abuse: the educational perspective*, Oxford, Basil Blackwell.

MATTHEWS, H. (1987) 'The place of withdrawal' in BOOTH, T., POTTS, P. and SWANN, W. (eds) *Preventing Difficulties in Learning*, Oxford, Basil Blackwell/The Open University.

MILLER, J. and VAN LOON, B. (1982) *Darwin for Beginners*, London, Writers and Readers.

MONGON, D., HART, S., ACE, C. and RAWLINGS, A. (1989) *Improving Classroom Behaviour: new directions for teachers and pupils*, London, Cassell.

MORRIS, H. (1925) *Memorandum on Village Colleges*, Cambridge, Cambridge University Press.

MORTON, J. (1994) *A Guide to the Criminal Justice and Public Order Act 1994*, London, Butterworths.

NAVA, M. (1988) 'Cleveland and the press: outrage and anxiety in the reporting of child sexual abuse', *Feminist Review*, **28**, pp. 103–21.

POTTS, P., ARMSTRONG, F. and MASTERTON, M. (eds) (1995a) *Equality and Diversity in Education 1: learning, teaching and managing in schools*, London, Routledge.

POTTS, P., ARMSTRONG, F. and MASTERTON, M. (eds) (1995b) *Equality and Diversity in Education 2: national and international contexts*, London, Routledge.

PYE, J. (1990) *Invisible Children: who are the real losers at school?*, Oxford, Oxford University Press.

ROGERS, R. (1989) *HIV and AIDS: what every tutor needs to know*, London, Longman.

SEBBA, J., BYERS, R. and ROSE, R. (1993) *Redefining the Whole Curriculum for*

Pupils with Learning Difficulties, London, Fulton.

SEDGEWICK, F. (1988) 'Sort this one out ...', *Times Educational Supplement*, 28 October 1988.

SHARP, S. and SMITH, P. K. (1994) *Tackling Bullying in your School: a practical handbook for teachers*, London, Routledge.

SHOSTAK, J. (1983) *Maladjusted Schooling: deviance, social control and individuality in secondary schooling*, London, Falmer Press.

SMITH, P. K. and SHARP, S. (1994) *School Bullying: insights and perspectives*, London, Routledge.

SOCIAL SERVICES INSPECTORATE/OFFICE FOR STANDARDS IN EDUCATION (1995) *The Education of Children who are looked after by Local Authorities*, London, Department of Health/Office for Standards in Education.

STIRLING, M. (1992) 'How many pupils are being excluded?', *British Journal of Special Education*, **19**(4), 128–30.

TOMLINSON, S. (1981) *Educational Subnormality: a study in decision making*, London, Routledge and Kegan Paul.

WORLD HEALTH ORGANIZATION (1994) *Communicable Disease Report*, **4** (46), 18 November 1994.

WORLD HEALTH ORGANIZATION (1995) *Communicable Disease Report*, **5** (20), 18 May 1995.

ACKNOWLEDGEMENTS

Grateful acknowledgement is made to the following sources for permission to reproduce material in this unit:

Text

Page 10: Adams, A. (1990) 'Beaten by a head', *Guardian*, 19 June 1990; *page 11*: Hull, R. (1985) *The Language Gap*, Methuen & Co; *page 22*: Graves, R. (1995) 'Flying Crooked', *Centenary Selected Poems*, Carcanet Press Limited; *page 36*: Mongon, D., Hart, S., Ace, C. and Rawlings, A. (1989) *Improving Classroom Behaviour: new directions for teachers and pupils*, Cassell plc; *page 58*: Croall, J. (1991) 'Disability no drawback', *Times Educational Supplement*, 31 May 1991, Times Supplements Ltd; *page 62*: Sedgwick, F. (1988) 'Sort this one out', *Times Educational Supplement*, 28 October 1988, Times Supplements Ltd; *Appendix 1*: Mongon, D., Hart, S., Ace, C. and Rawlings, A. (1989) *Improving Classroom Behaviour: new directions for teachers and pupils*, Cassell plc.

Illustrations

Page 19: Professor Stephen Hawking at work, © MMP, Manni Mason's Pictures; *page 33:* from Miller, J. (1982) *Darwin for Beginners*, Writers and Readers Publishing Co-operative Society Ltd, illustration copyright © 1982 Borin Van Loon, reproduced by permission of Glen Thompson, Airlift; *page 67 (middle right):* TES, 17 May 1991, p. 22, Gillies Mackinnon; *page 67 (middle left):* TES, 3 May 1991, p. 12, Bill Stott; *page 67 (bottom):* TES2, 30 September 1994, p. 12, Nick Newman; *page 68 (top):* TES, 26 June 1992, p. 87, Breakdown, Jeremy Long; *page 68 (middle):* TES, 25 June 1993, p. 20, Bill Stott; *page 68 (bottom):* TES, 27 January 1995, p. 20, Breakdown, Jeremy Long; *page 69 (top):* TES, 31 July 1992, p. 12, Bill Stott; *page 69 (bottom):* TES, 14 June 1991, p. 24, Nigel Paige.

E242 UNIT TITLES

Unit 1/2   Making Connections

Unit 3/4   Learning from Experience

Unit 5   Right from the Start

Unit 6/7   Classroom Diversity

Unit 8/9   Difference and Distinction

Unit 10   Critical Reading

Unit 11/12   Happy Memories

Unit 13   Further and Higher

Unit 14/15   Power in the System

Unit 16   Learning for All